THE ARABIC ALPHABET

SOUND	LETTER	NAME
r	ر	raw
z	ز	zay
s	س	seen
sh	ش	sheen
sw	ص	sawd
dw	ض	dawd
tw	ط	taw
zw	ظ	zaw
'a	ع	ayn

SOUND	LETTER	NAME
a	ا	alif
b	ب	ba
t	ت	ta
th	ث	tha
j	ج	jeem
H	ح	Ha
kh	خ	kha
d	د	dal
dh	ذ	dhal

...CONTINUED

SOUND	LETTER	NAME
m	م	meem
n	ن	noon
h	ه	ha
w	و	wow
y	ي	ya

SOUND	LETTER	NAME
g	غ	gayn
f	ف	fa
q	ق	qaf
k	ك	kaf
l	ل	lam

PRONUNCIATION CHART

a	ا	a as in **a**pple
b	ب	b as in **b**at
t	ت	t as in **t**ap
th	ث	tha as in **th**ing
j	ج	j as in **j**am
H	ح	H is a heavy H
kh	خ	kh like cough pronounced from the throat
d	د	d as in **d**ad
dh	ذ	dh as in **th**ere
r	ر	r as in zo**rr**o, slightly rolled
z	ز	z as in **z**ebra
s	س	s as in **s**ing
sh	ش	sh as in **sh**ape

sw	ص	saw as in **saw**
dw	ض	daw as in **daw**n
tw	ط	taw as in **tau**ght
zw	ظ	zaw as in **zaw**
'e	ع	e as in **e**ye
g	غ	g as in **g**uy
f	ف	f as in **f**amily
q	ق	q as in **q**uarter
k	ك	k as in **k**ite
l	ل	l as in **l**augh
m	م	m as in **m**ake
n	ن	n as in **n**oon
h	ه	h as in **ha**ppy
w	و	w as in **w**ow
y	ي	y as in **y**ou

HEAR THE DIFFERENCE ?

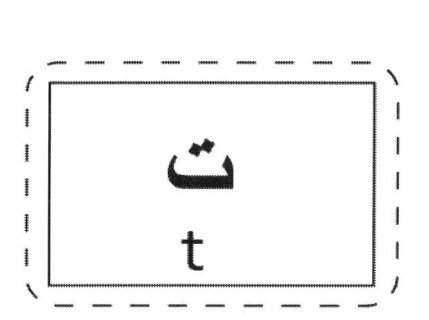

ت t	vs.	ط taw
t		1. hard like the t in taught. 2. carries a low 'w' sound 3. formed by touching the top of the tip of tongue to the back of the top two front teeth

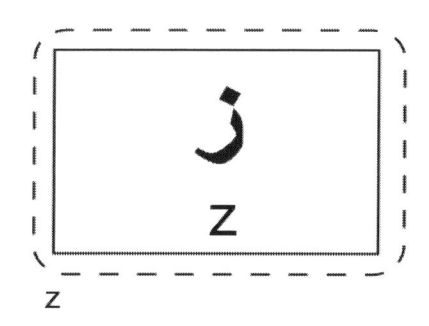

ز z	vs.	ظ zaw
z		1. hard z. 2. carries a low 'w' sound 3. formed by touching the left side of the tongue to the left teeth

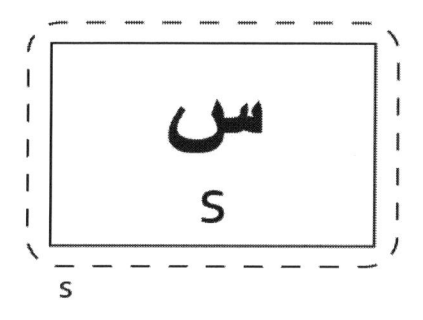

س s	vs.	ص saw
s		1. hard like the s in saw. 2. carries a low 'w' sound

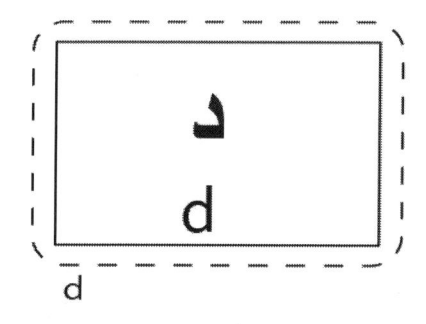

د d	vs.	ض daw
d		1. hard like the d in dog. 2. carries a low 'w' sound

HEAR THE DIFFERENCE?

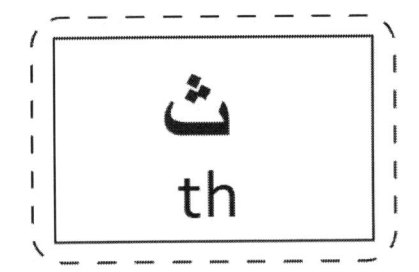

ث th vs. ذ th

formed by touching the top of the tip of the tongue to the bottom tip of the two front teeth

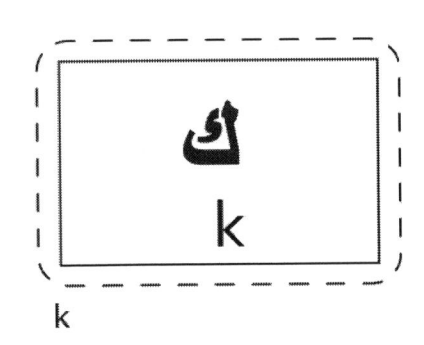

formed by touching the top of the tip of tongue to the back of the top two front teeth

ك k vs. خ kh

k

exhaled k from the throat

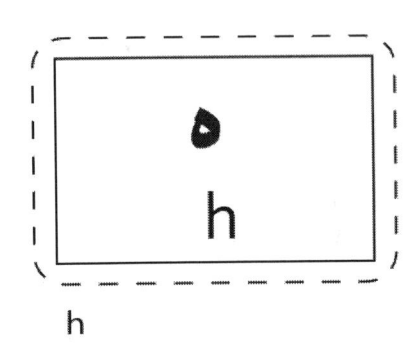

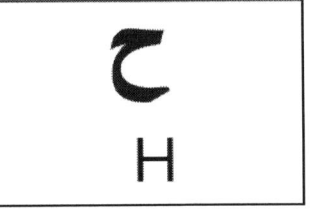

ه h vs. ح H

h

exhaled H from the throat

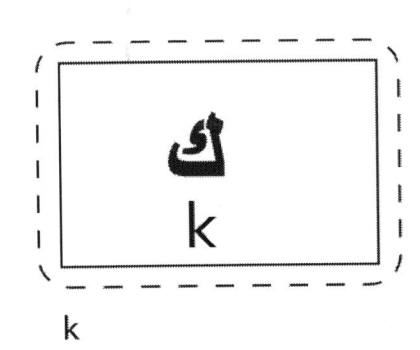

ك k vs. ق q

k

q

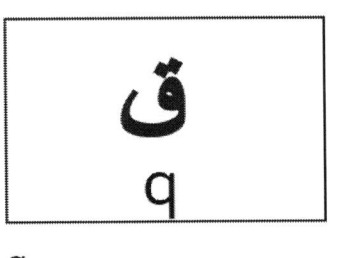

Lesson: 1

How to write it:
Begin at the top. Complete the letter in a single downward stroke.

Alif (a)

Guided Practice

Guided Practice

Guided Practice

Guided Practice

Lesson: 2

How to write it:
Begin at the right tip of the letter. Follow the arrows down, across to the left and back up. Finish with one dot centered under the letter.

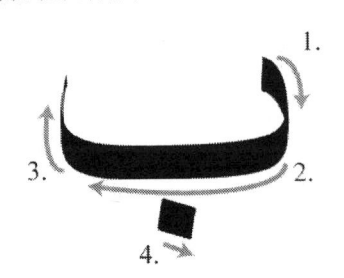

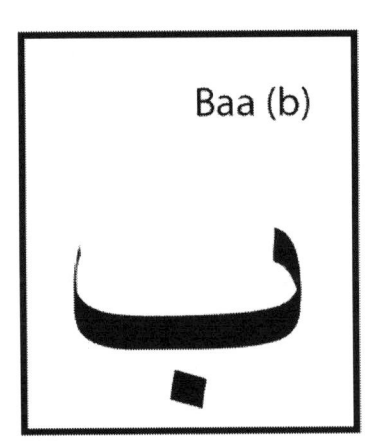

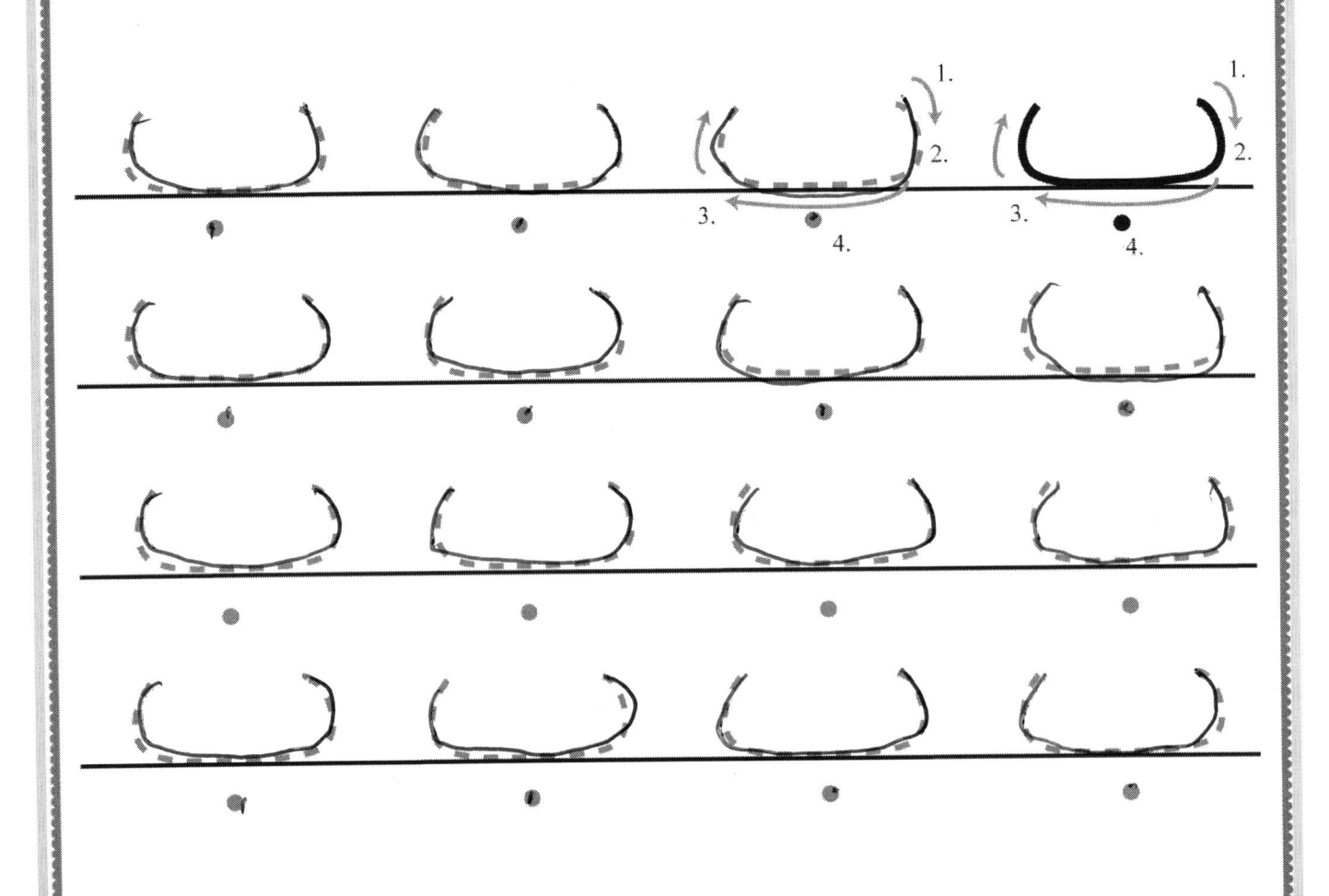

Baa (b)

ب

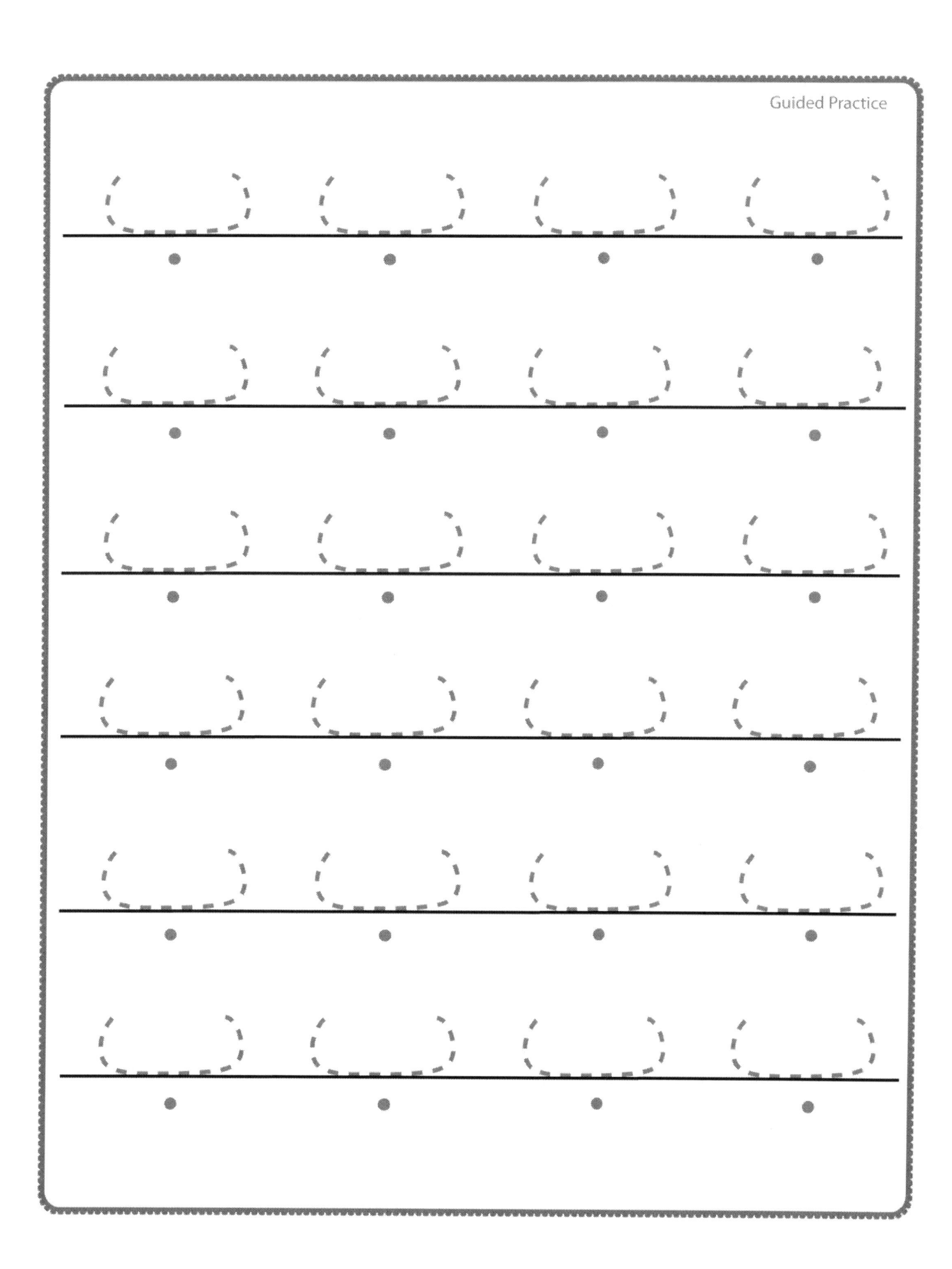

Guided Practice

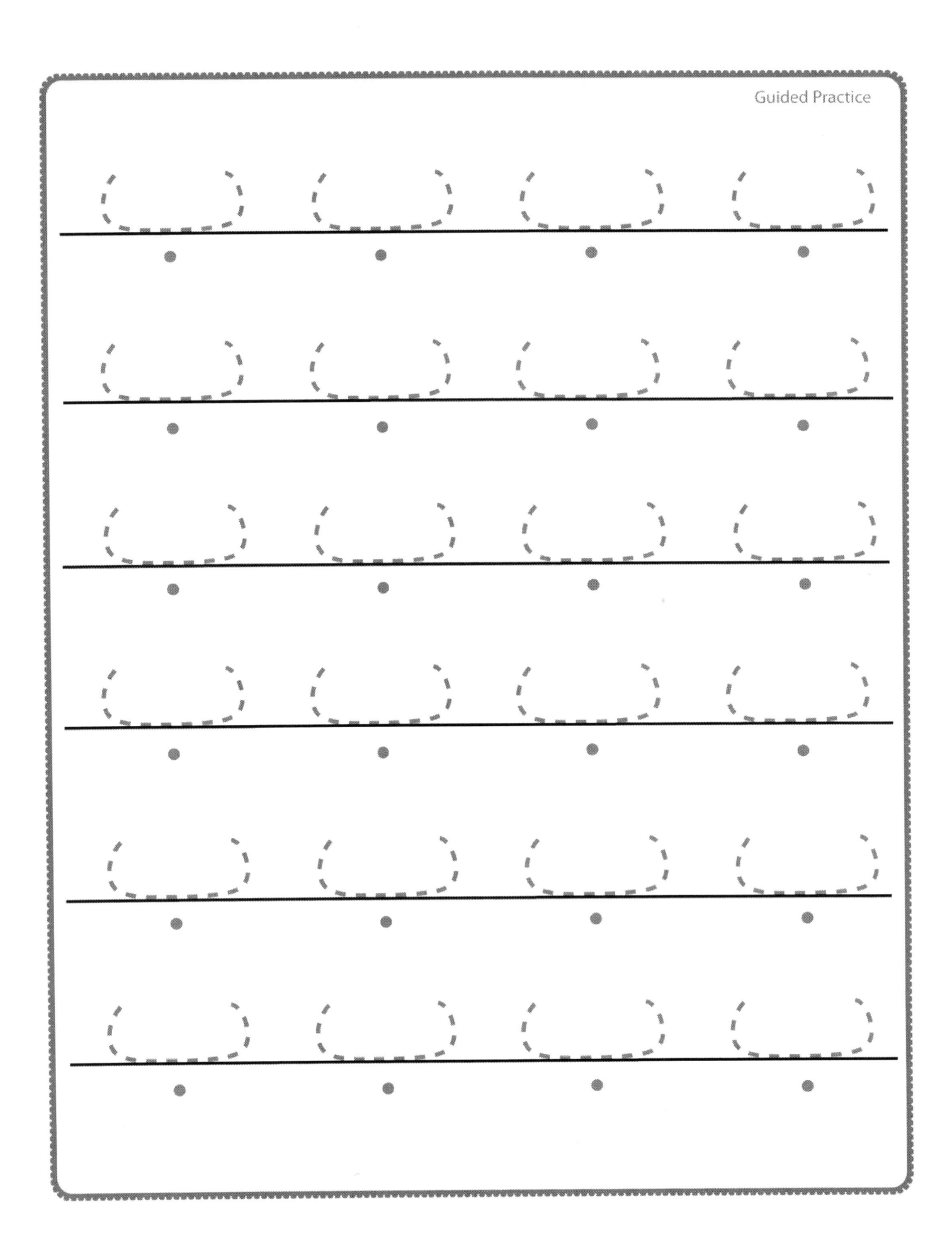

Guided Practice

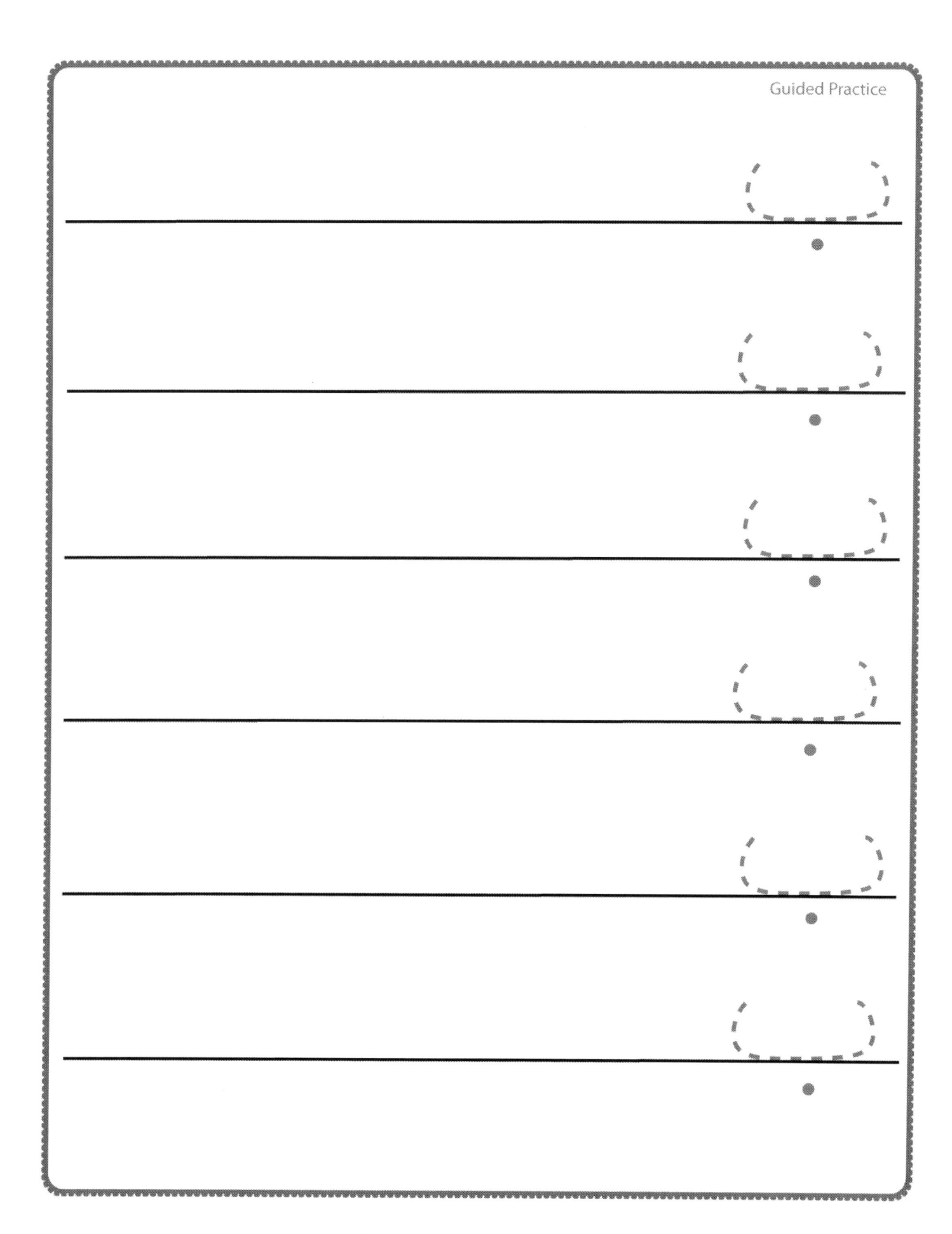

Guided Practice

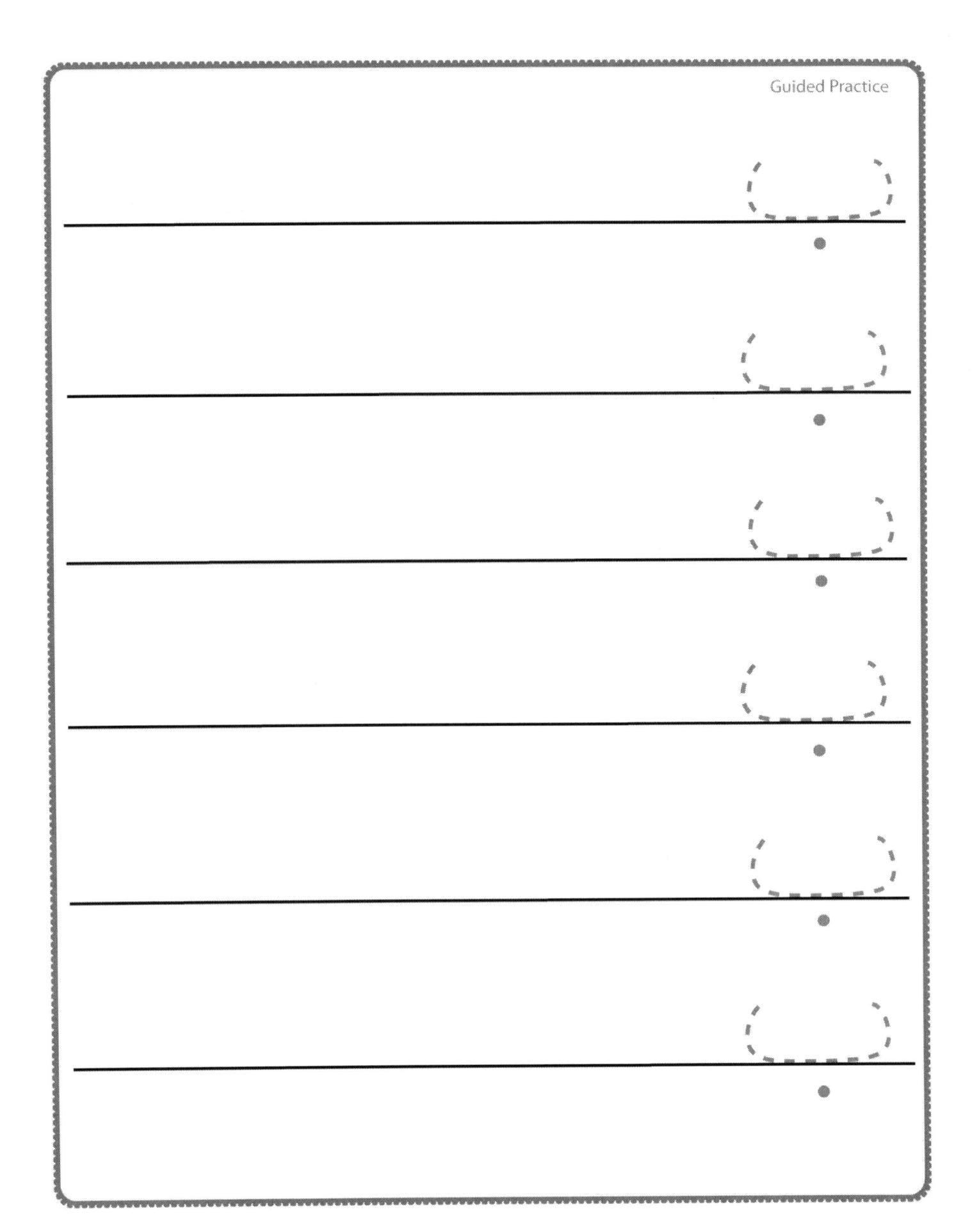

Guided Practice

Lesson: 3

How to write it:
Begin at the right tip of the letter. Follow the arrows down, across to the left and back up. Finish with two dots above the letter.

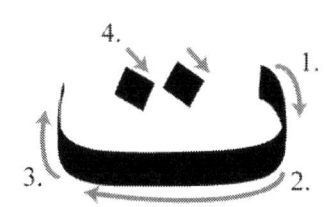

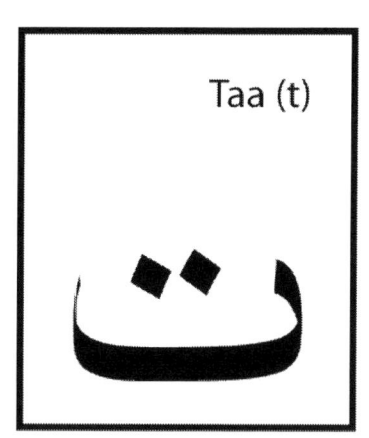

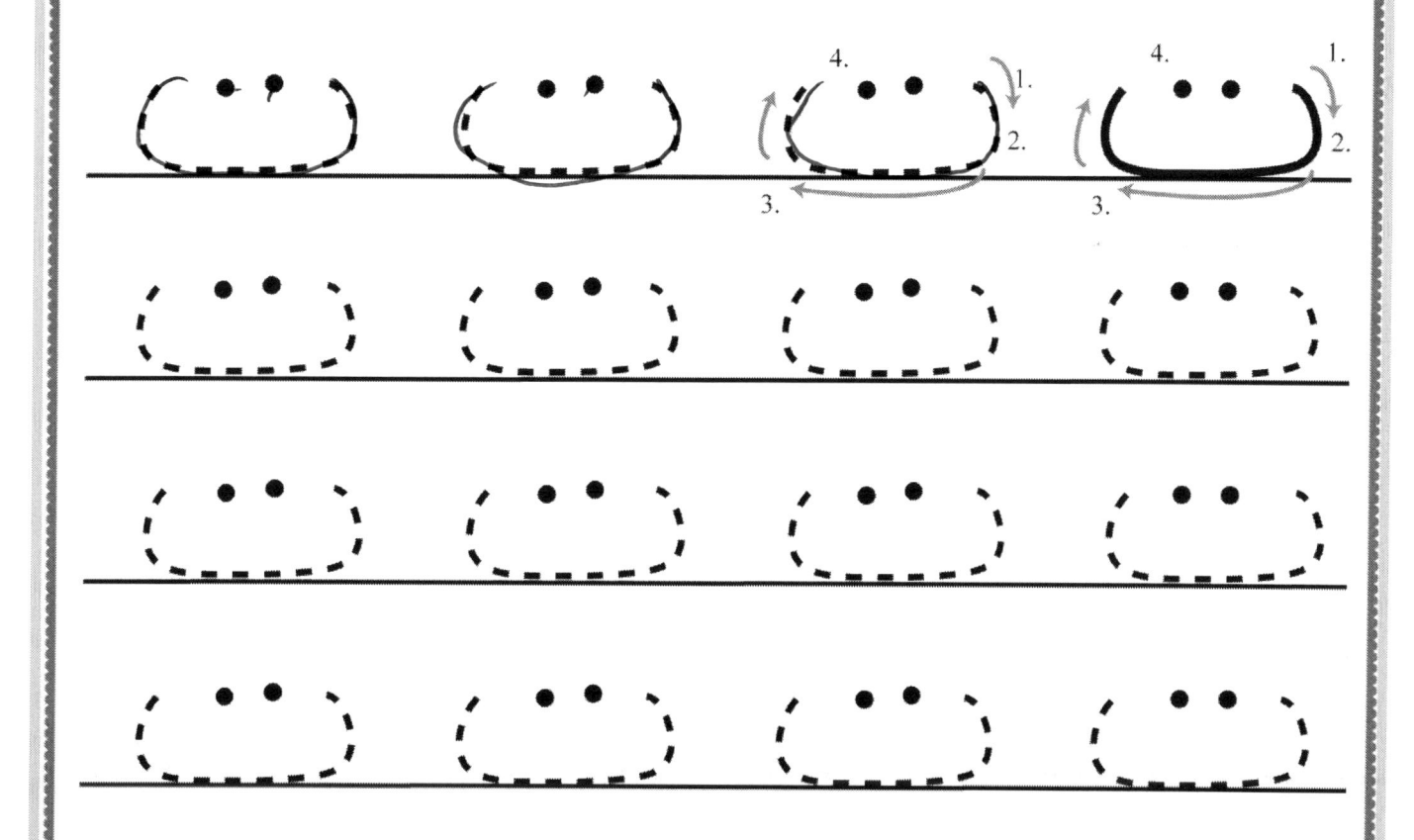

Taa (t)

ت

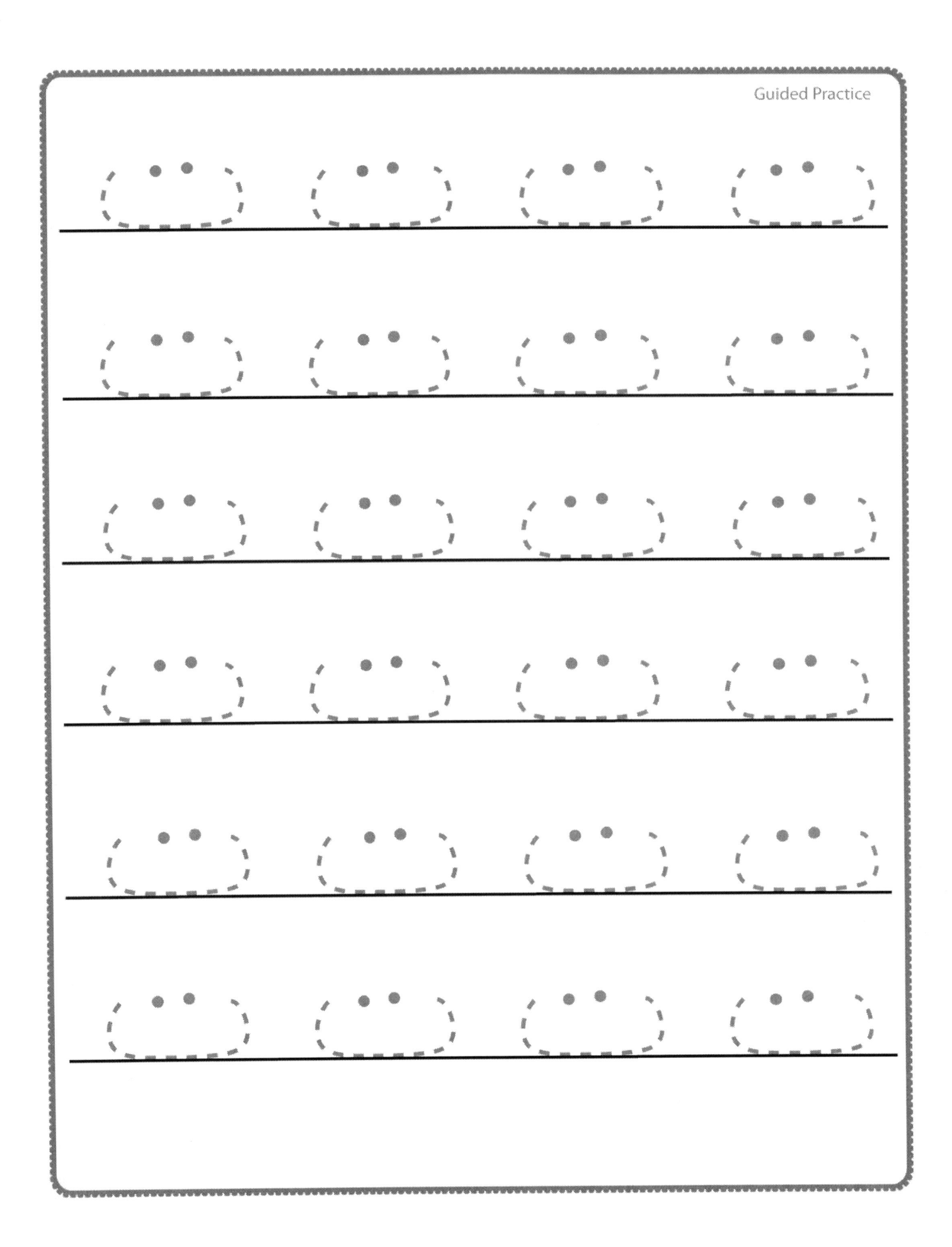

Guided Practice

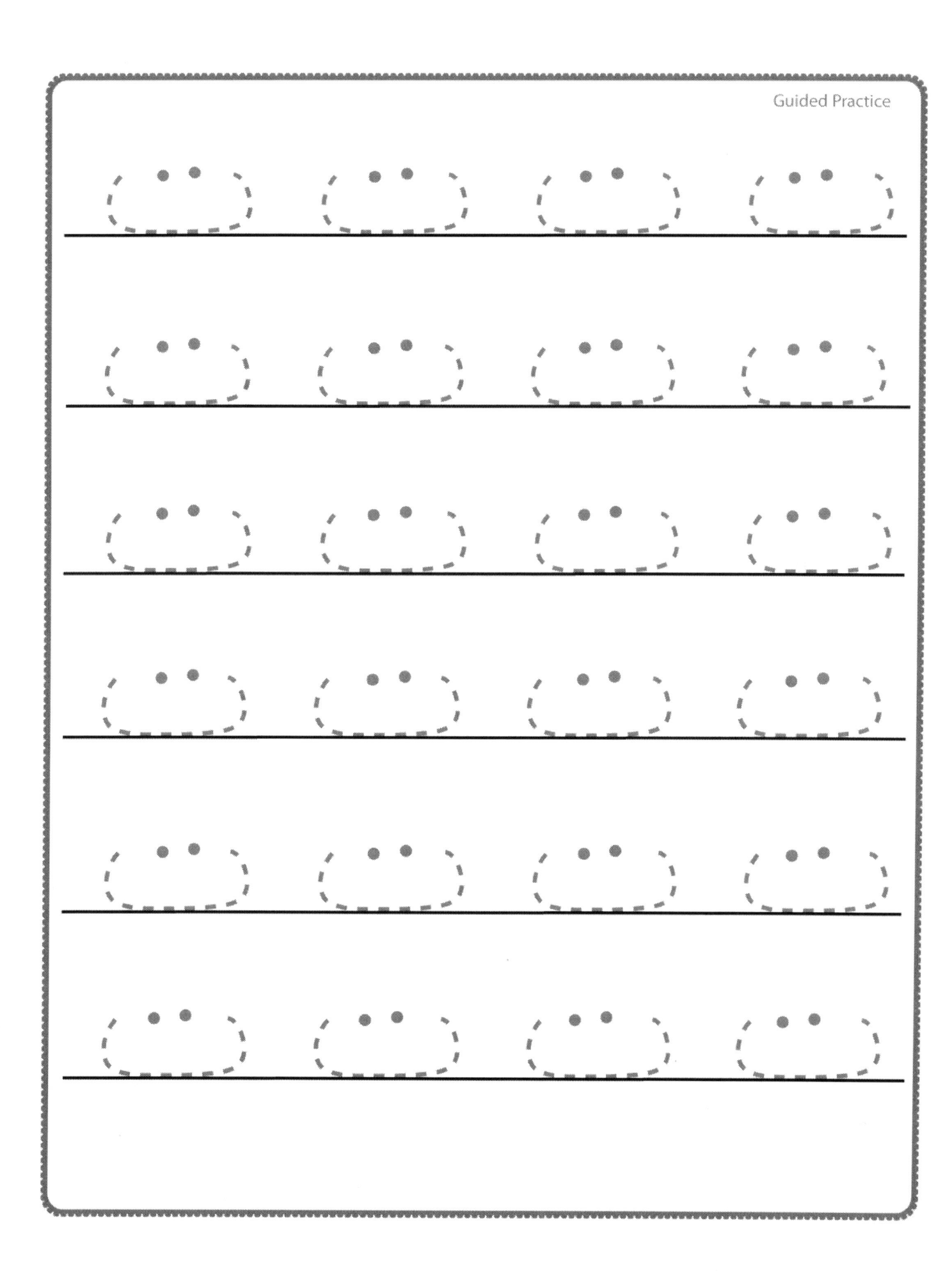

Guided Practice

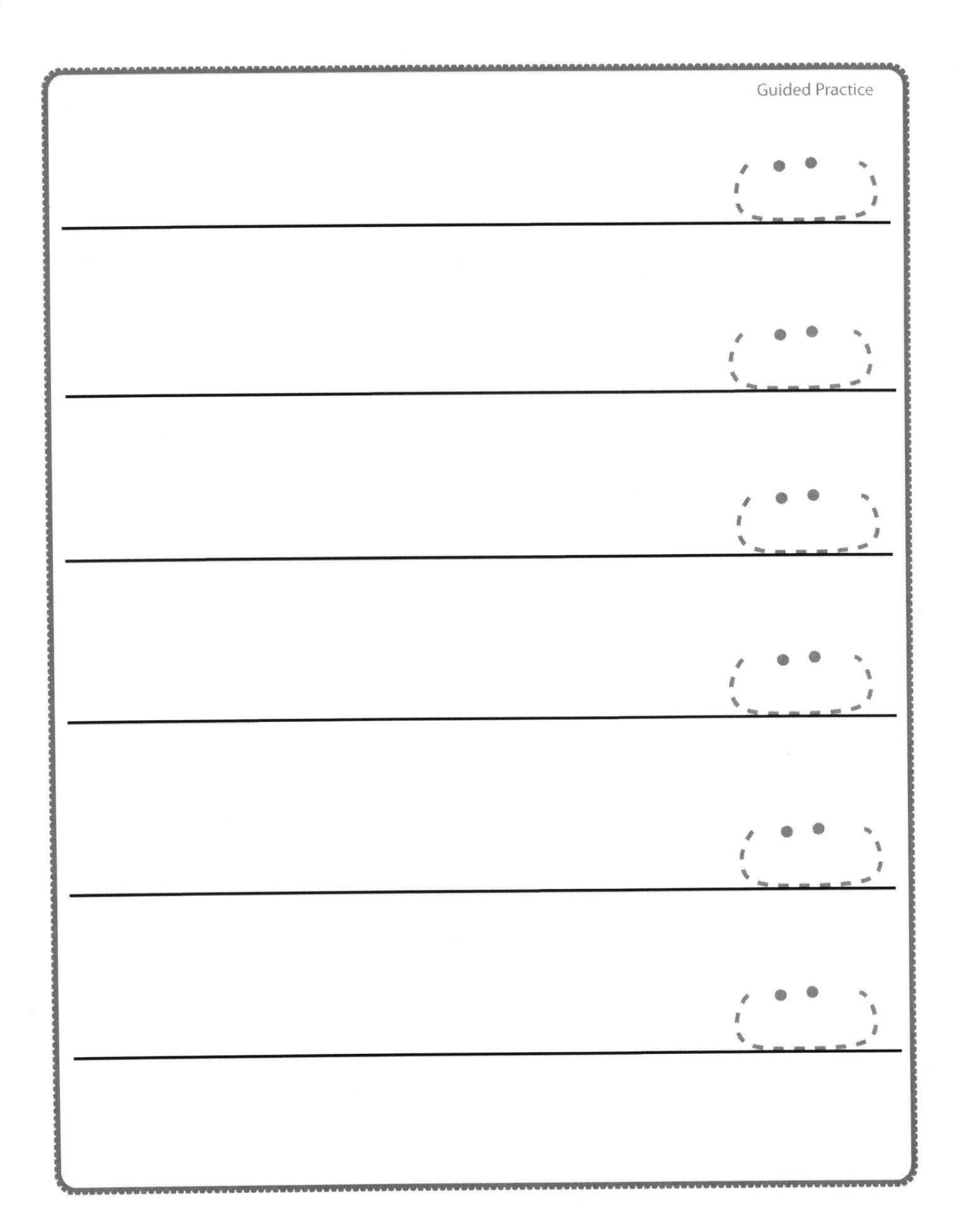

Guided Practice

Guided Practice

How to write it:
Begin at the right tip of the letter. Follow the arrows down, across to the left and back up. Finish with three dots above the letter.

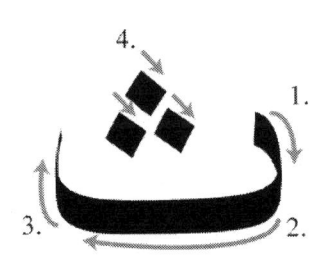

Thaa (th)

Lesson: 4

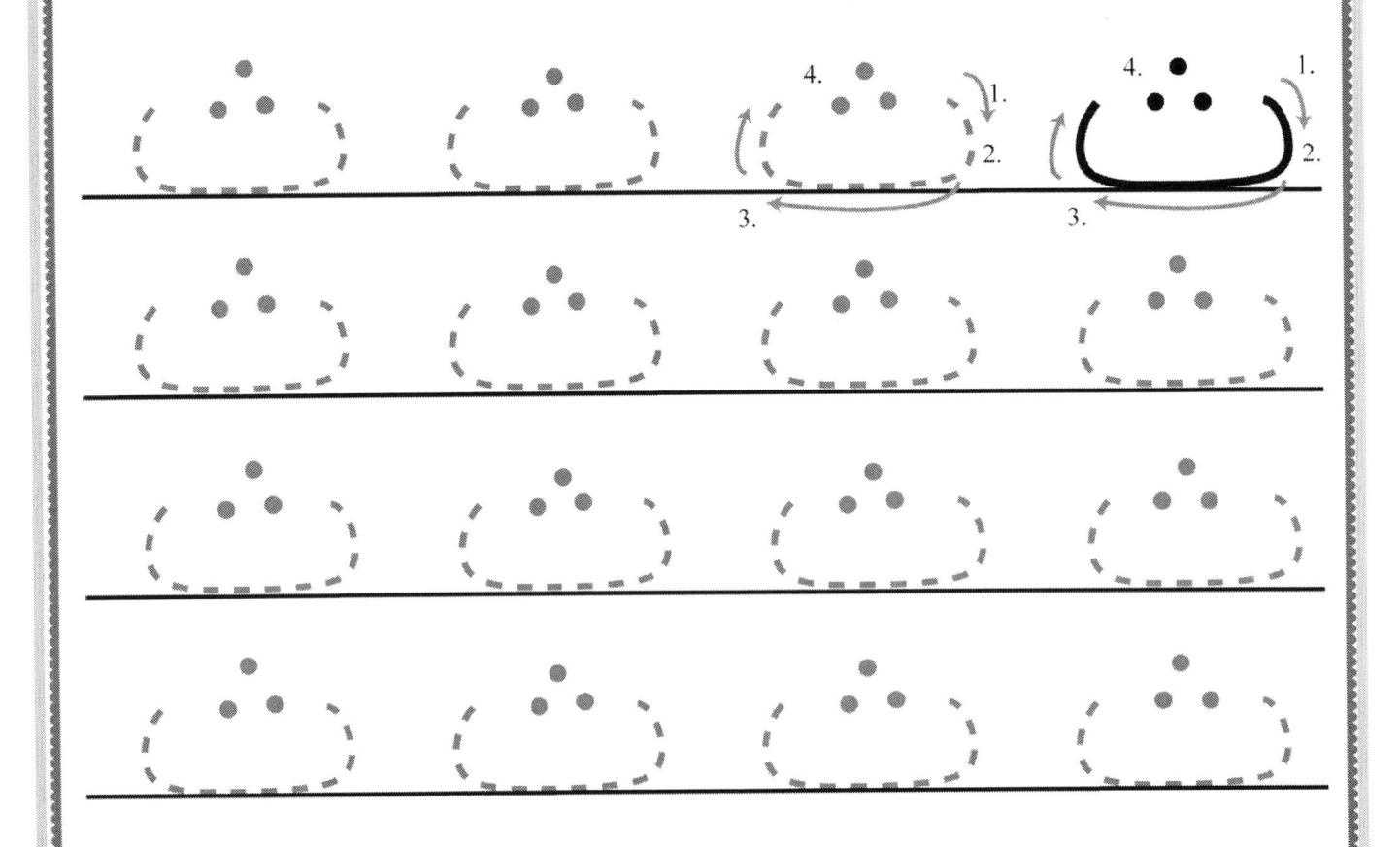

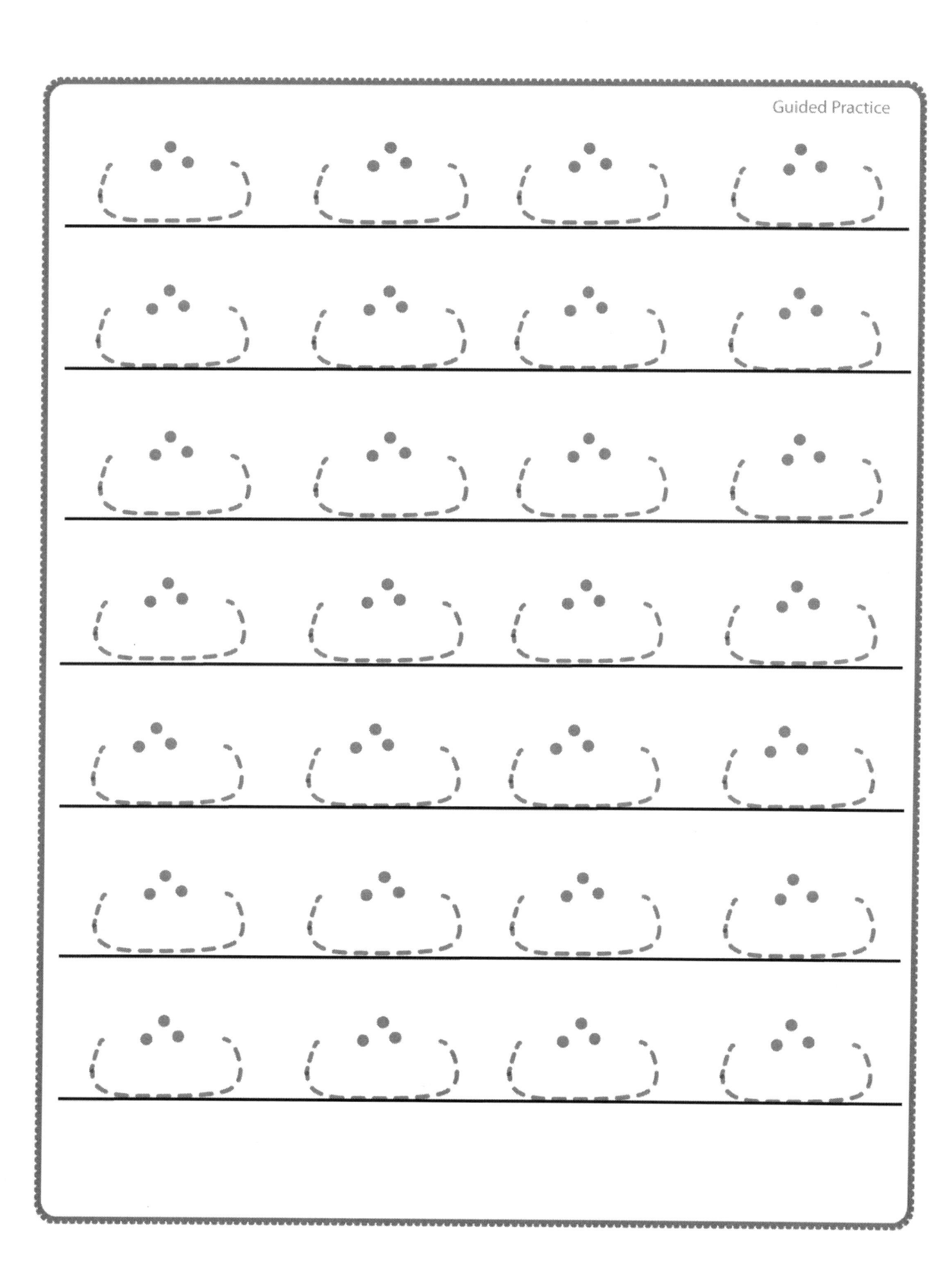

Guided Practice

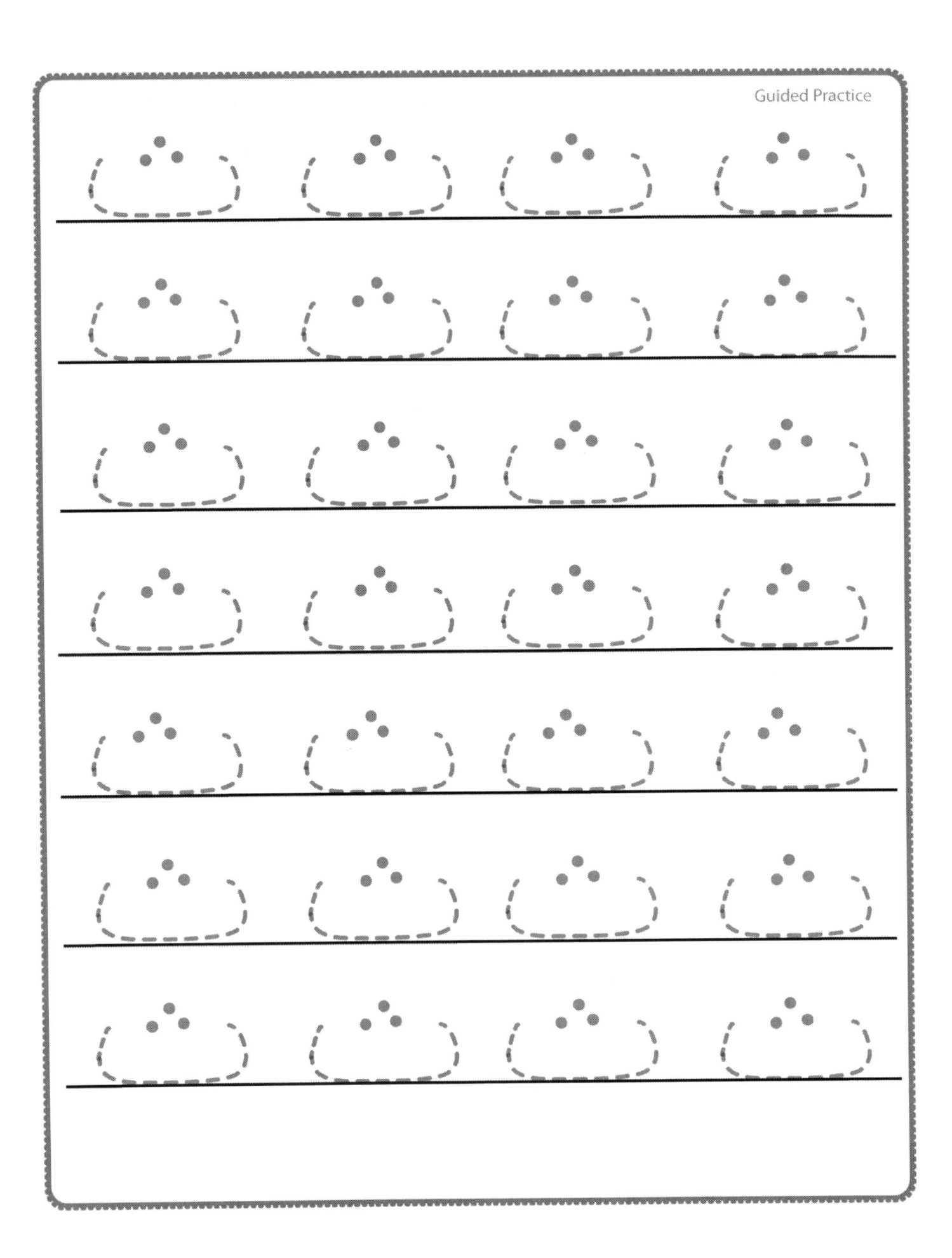

Guided Practice

Guided Practice

Guided Practice

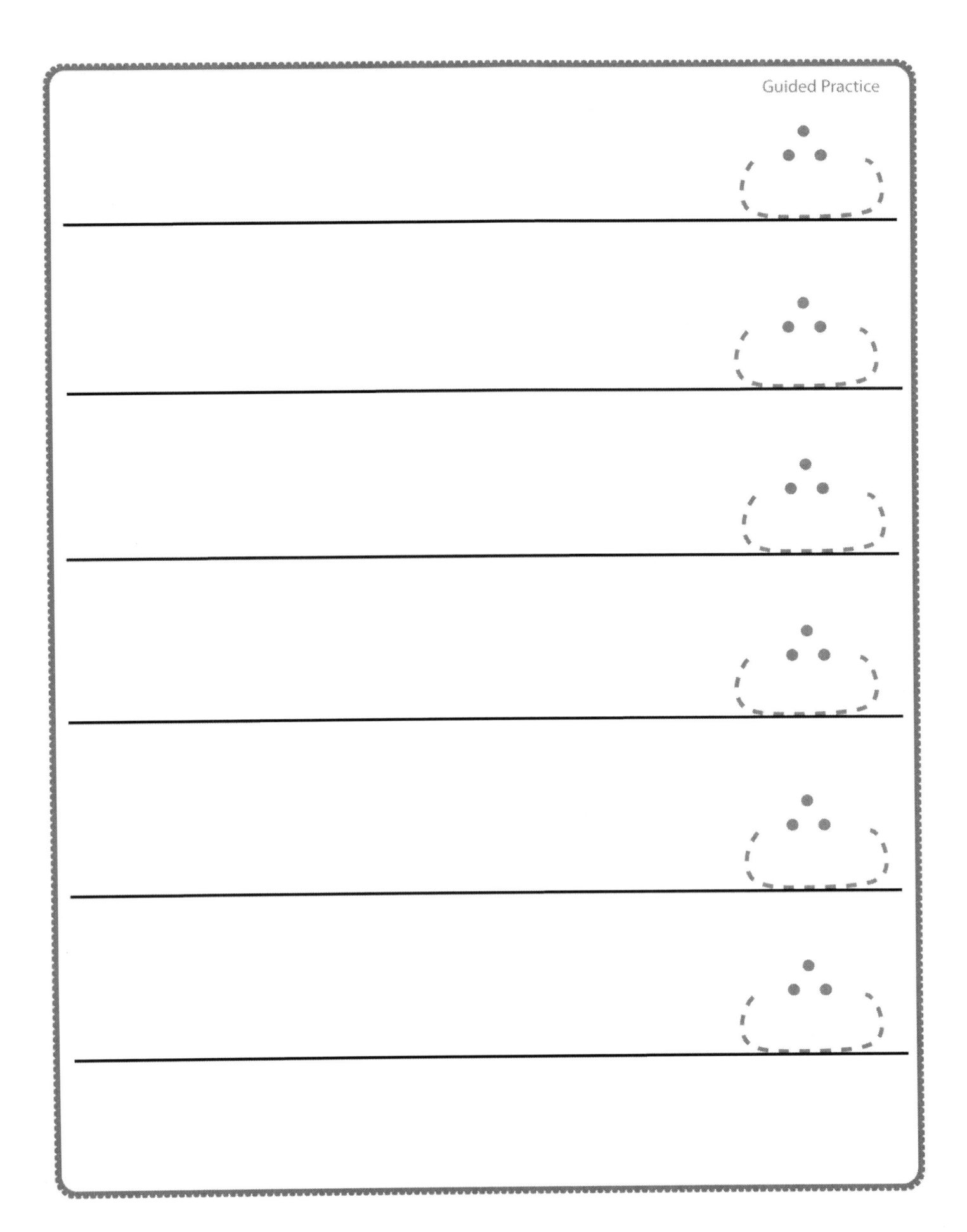

Lesson: 5

How to write it:
Most of this letter lies under the line. Begin at the left and follow the arrow across to the right. Now curve down and around the tail end. Draw a dot inside the curve.

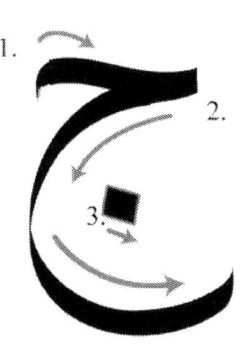

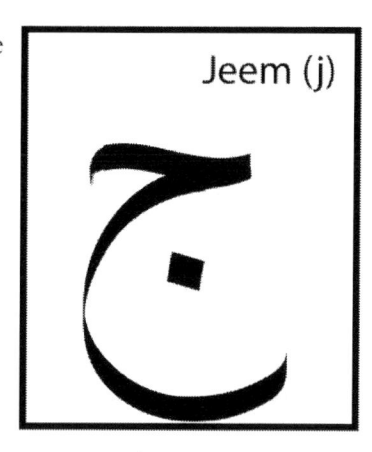

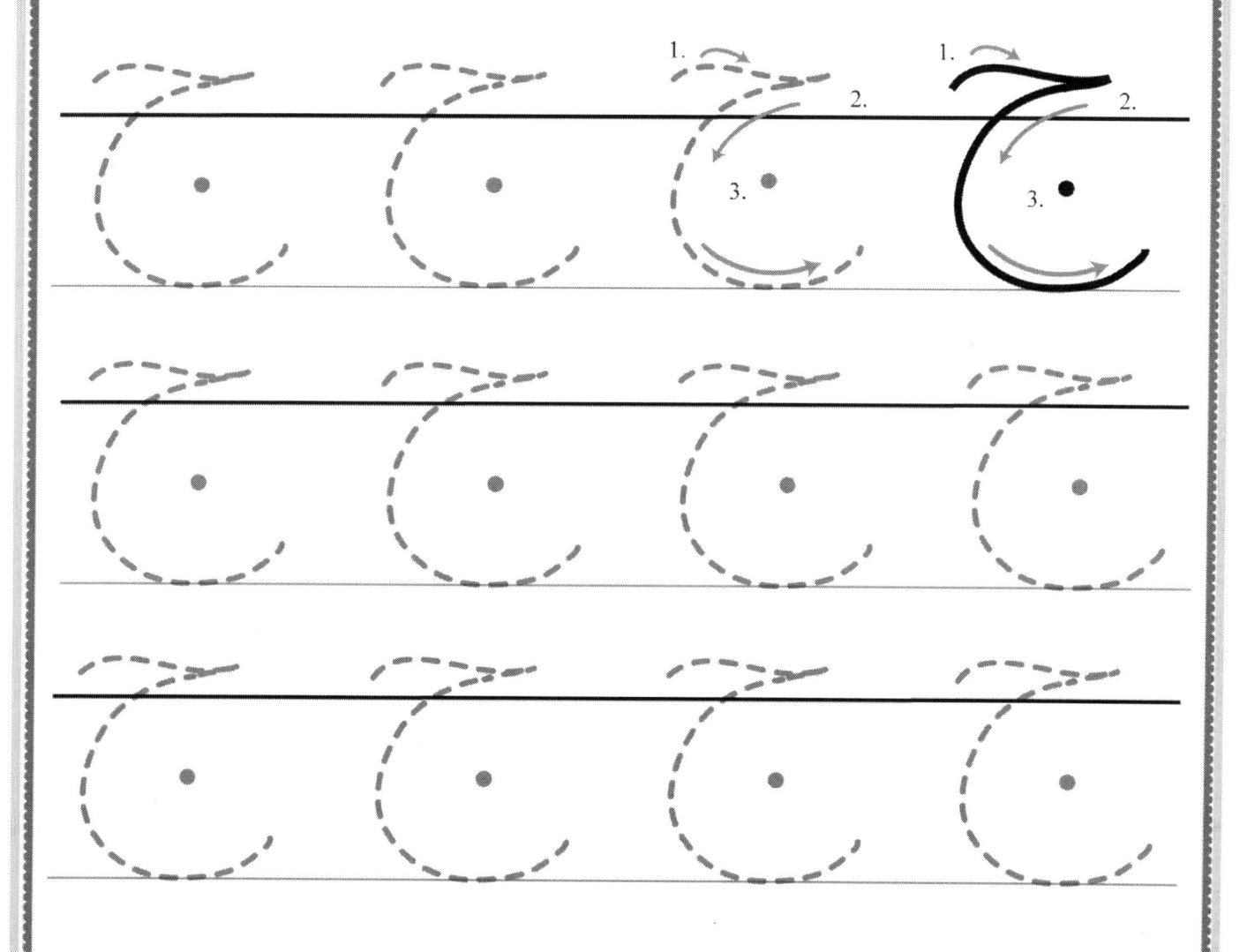

Jeem (j)

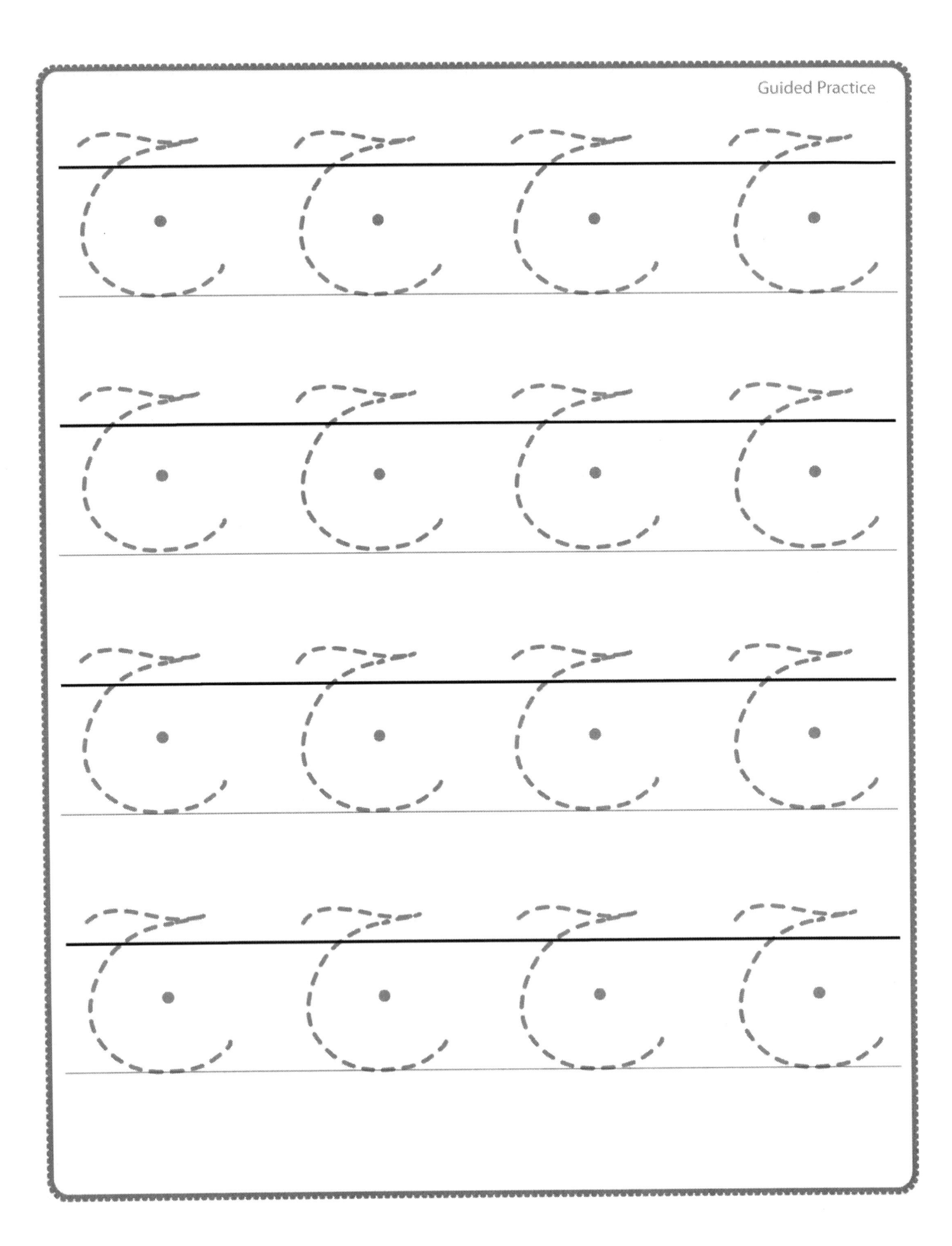

Guided Practice

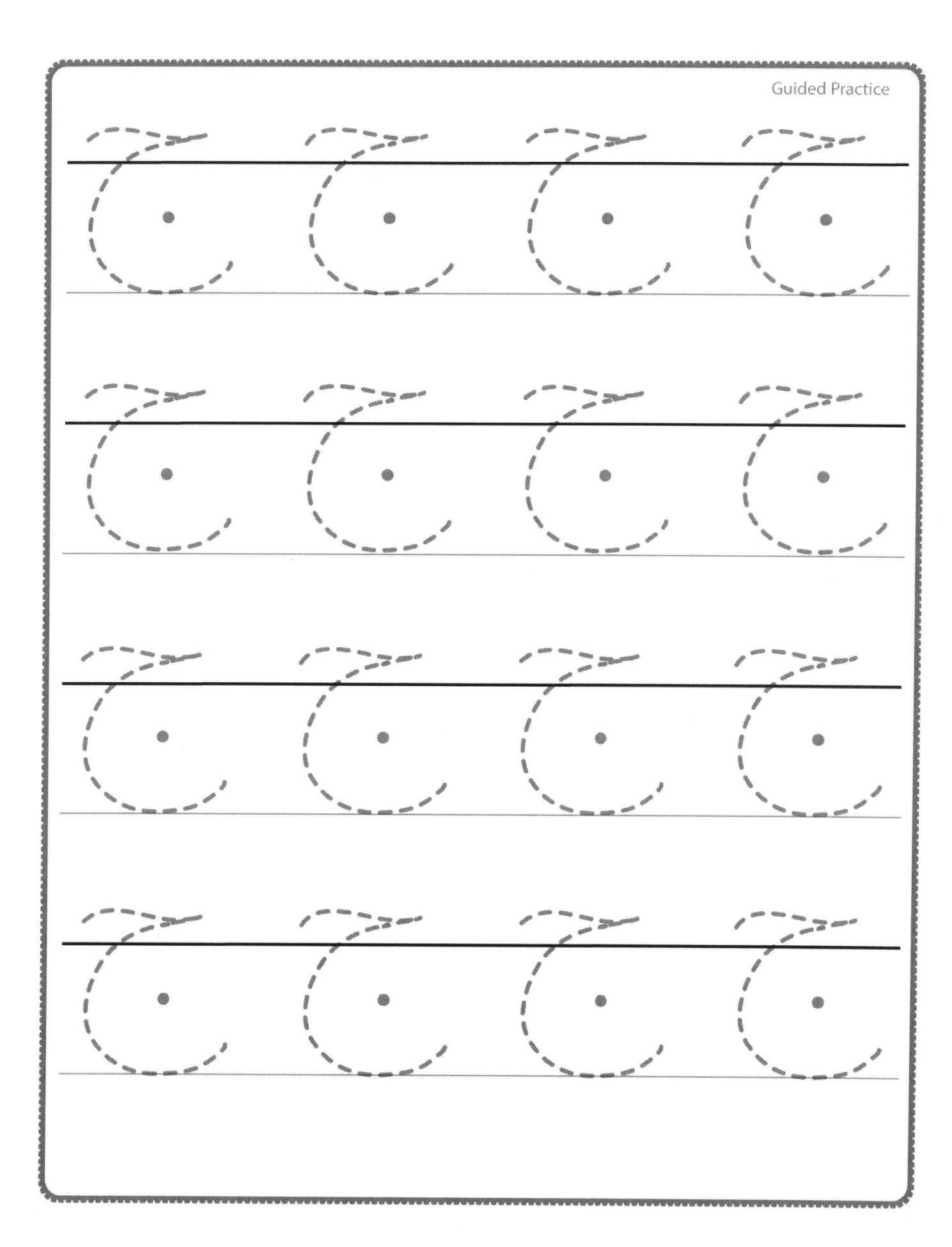

Guided Practice

Guided Practice

Guided Practice

Lesson: 6

How to write it:
Most of this letter lies under the line. Begin at the left and follow the arrow across to the right. Now curve down and around the tail end.

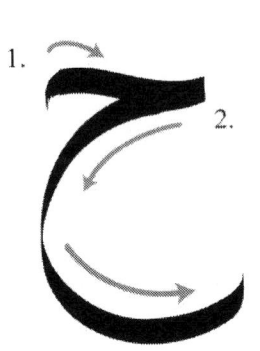

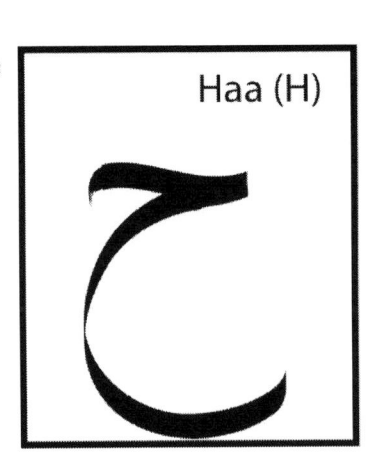

Haa (H)

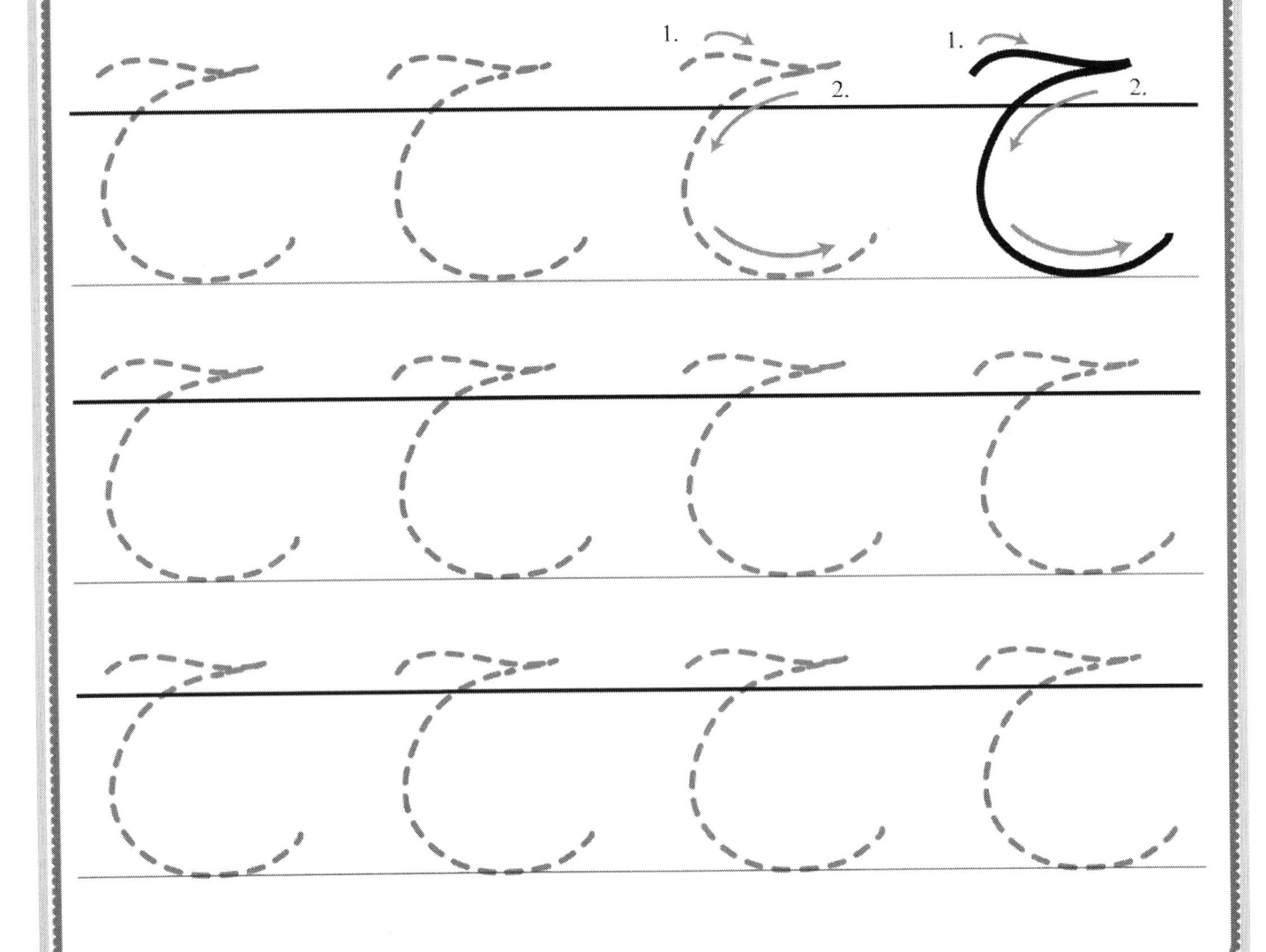

Guided Practice

Guided Practice

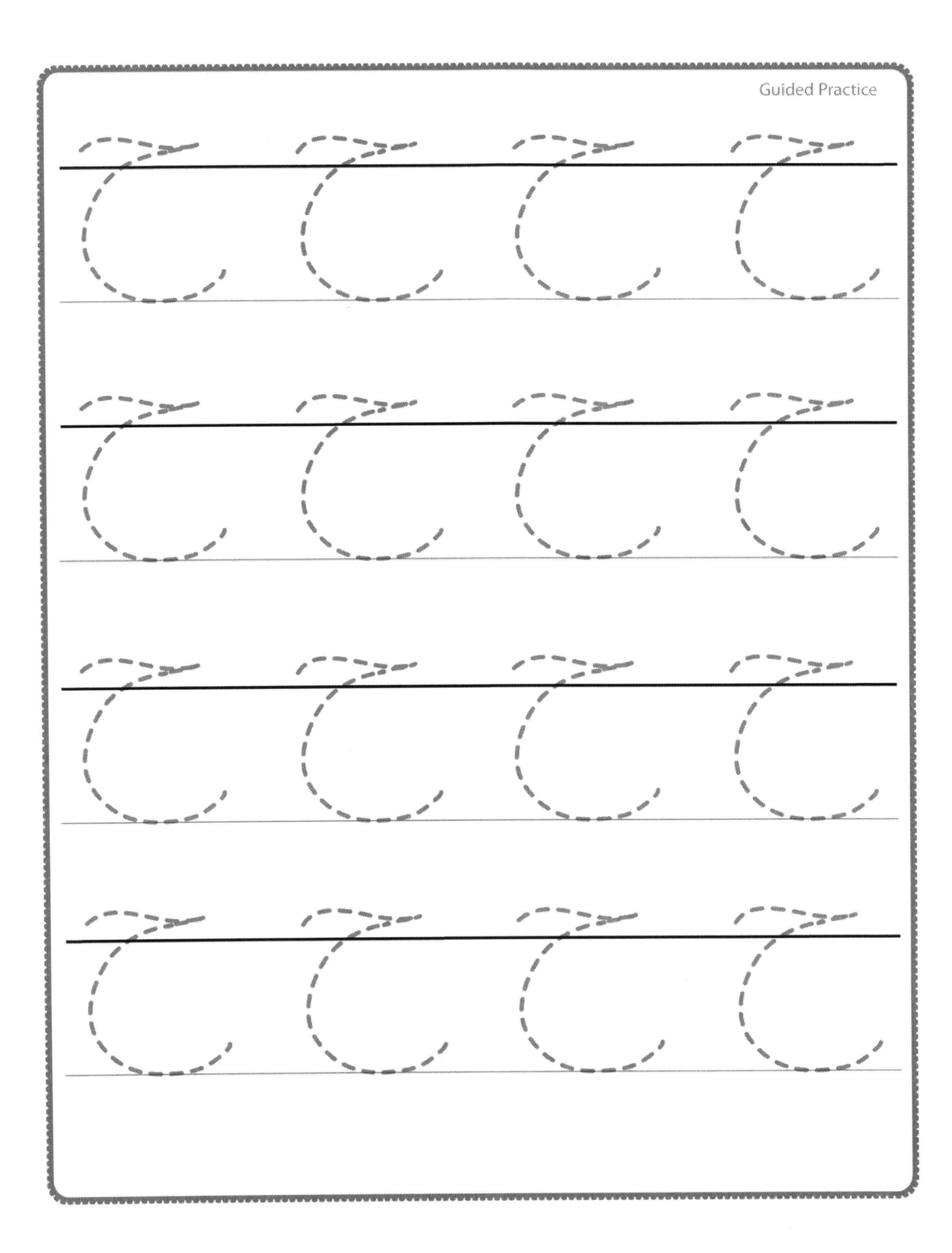

Guided Practice

Guided Practice

Lesson: 7

How to write it:
Most of this letter lies under the line. Begin at the left and follow the arrow across to the right. Now curve down and around the tail end. Draw a dot above the letter.

Khaa (kh)

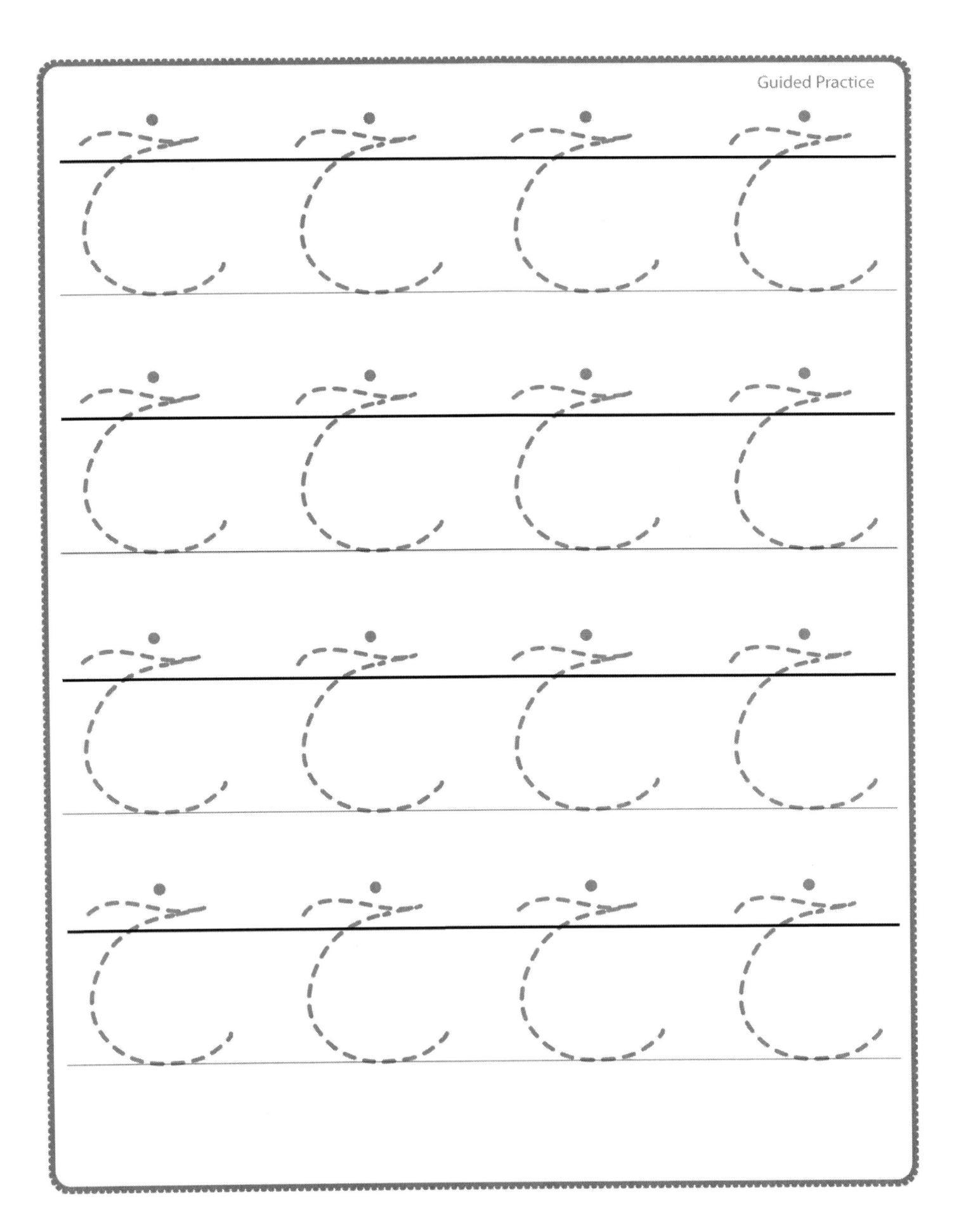

Guided Practice

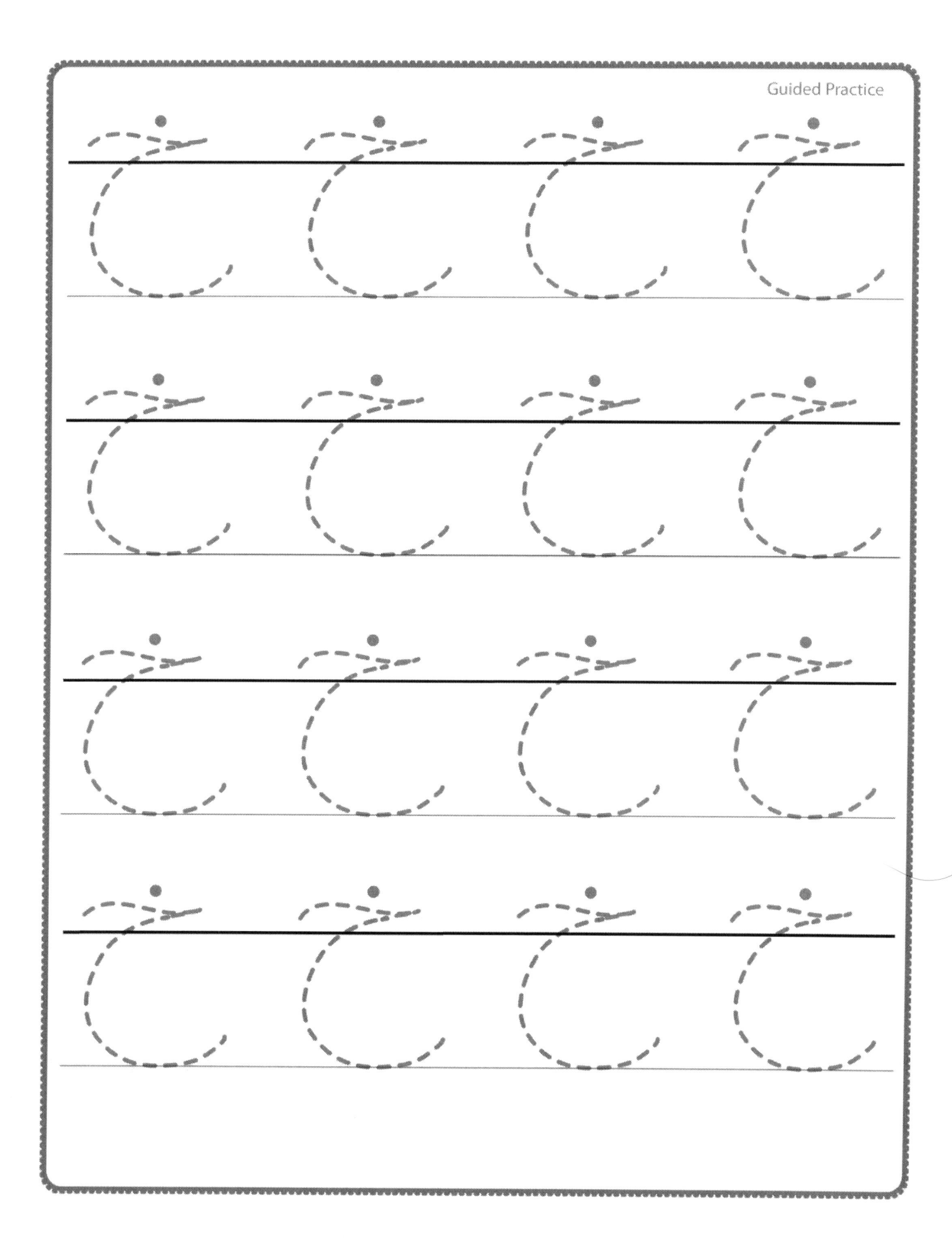

Guided Practice

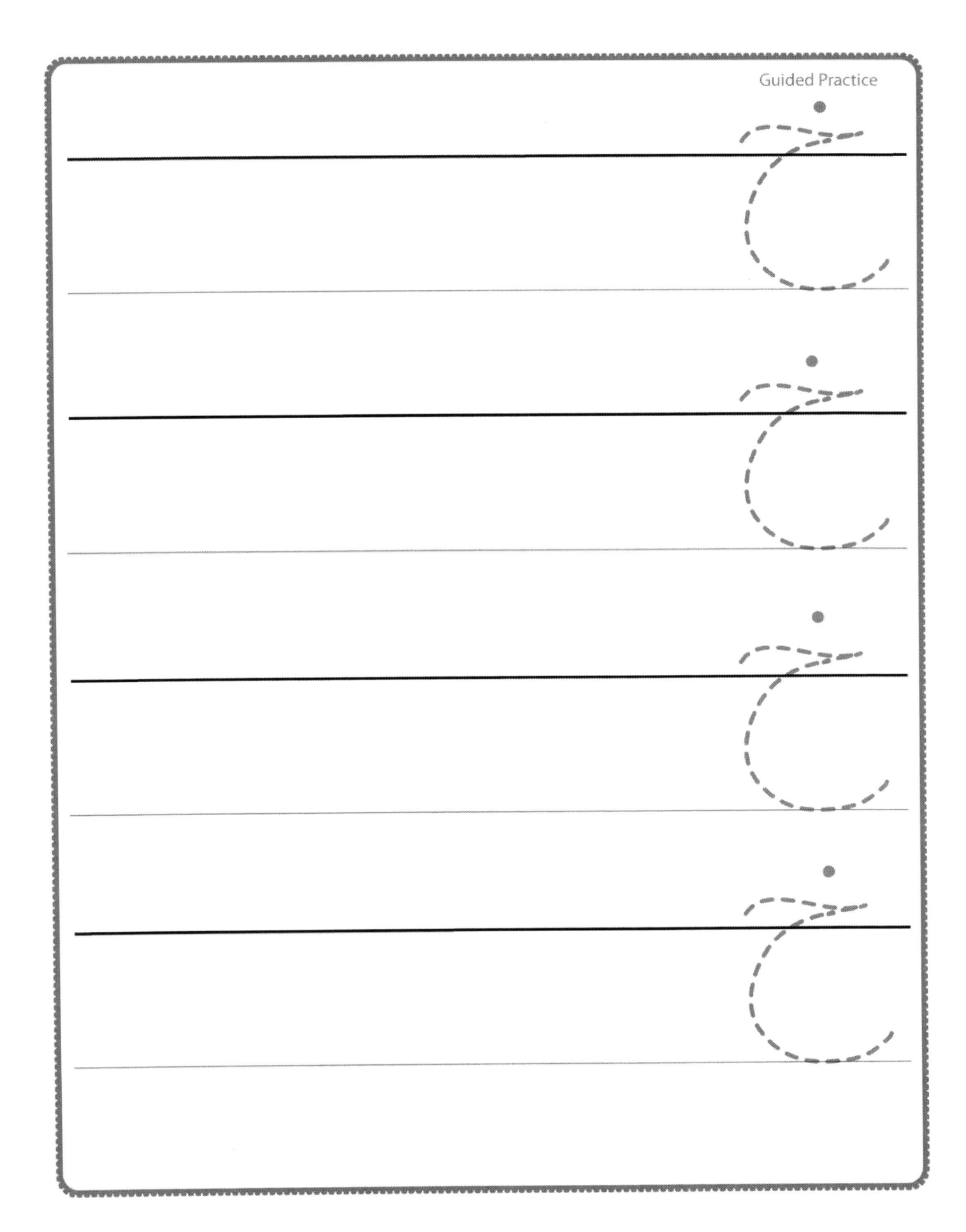

Guided Practice

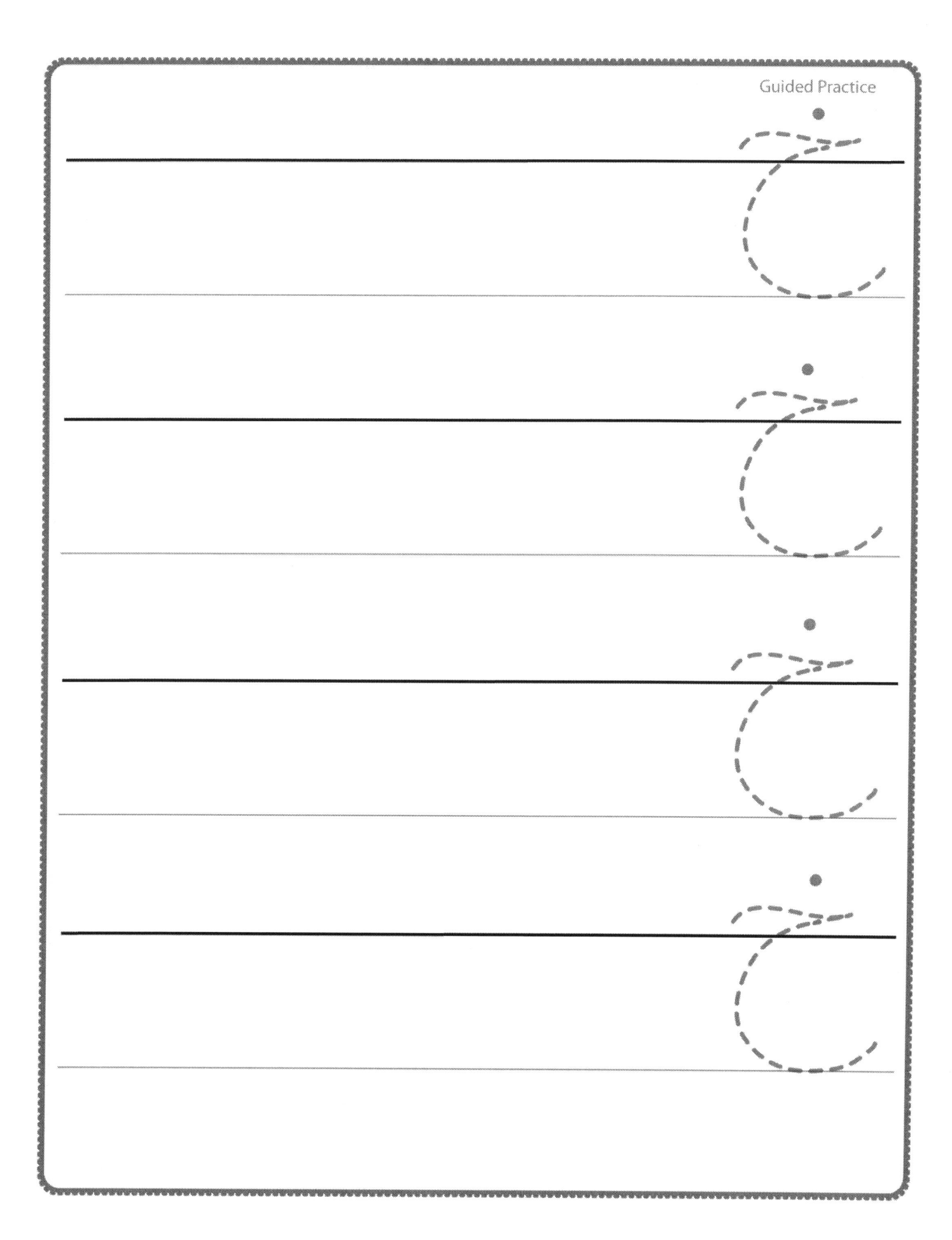

Guided Practice

Lesson: 8

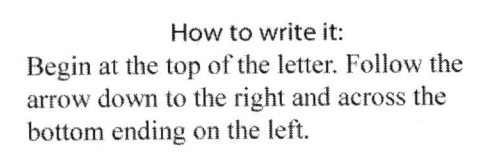

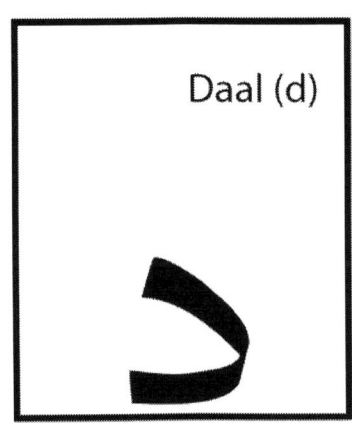

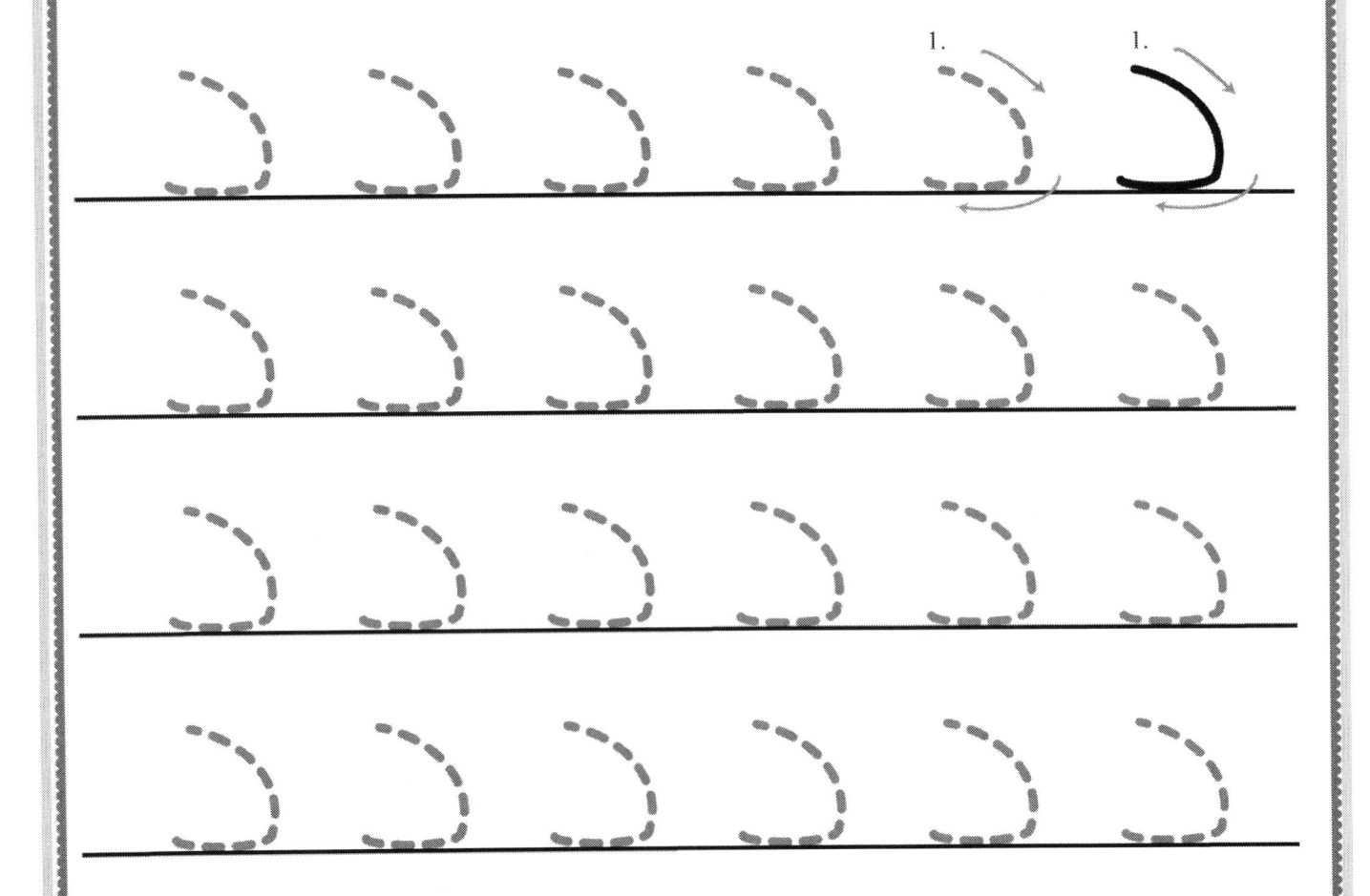

How to write it:
Begin at the top of the letter. Follow the arrow down to the right and across the bottom ending on the left.

Daal (d)

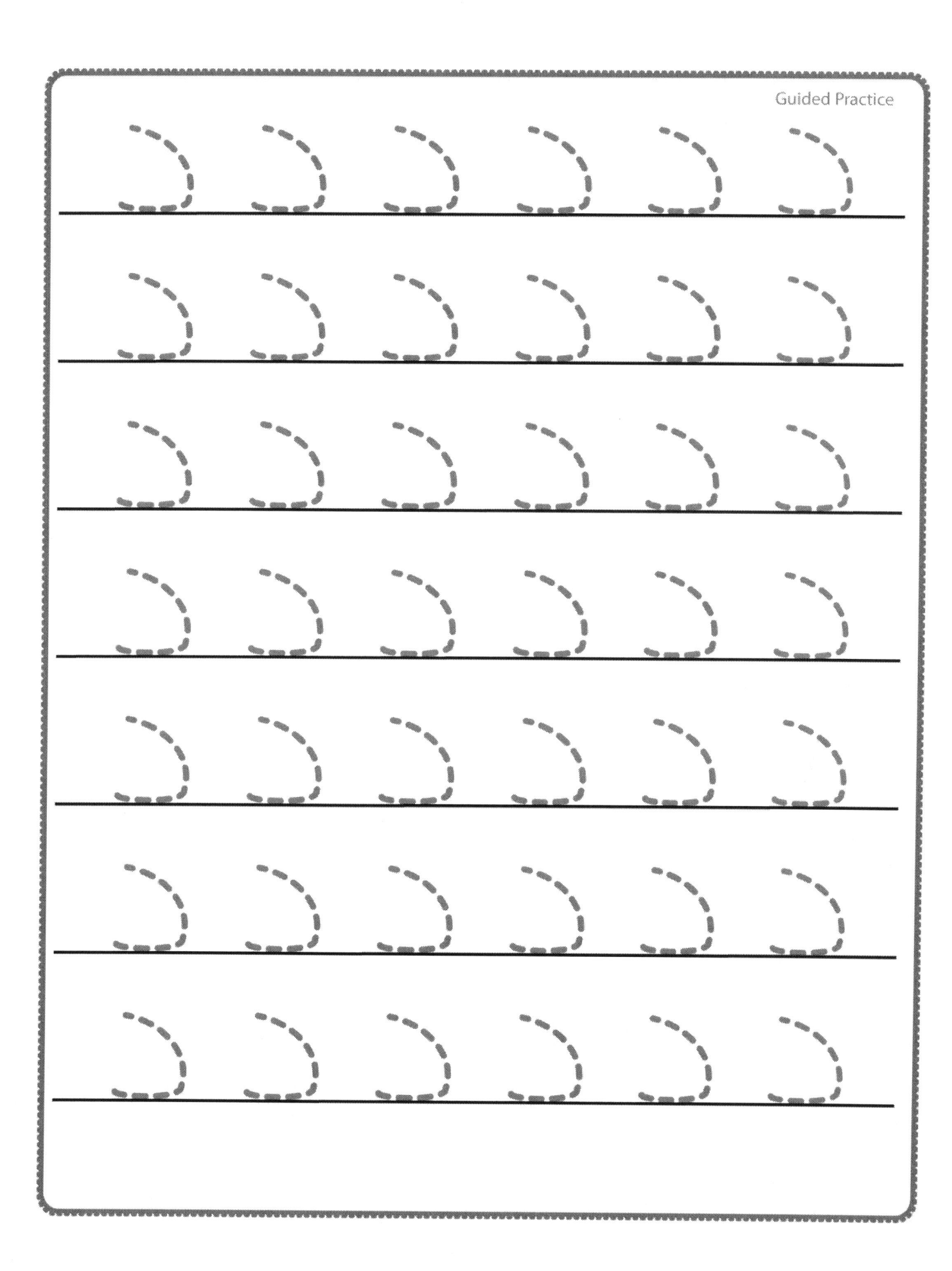

Guided Practice

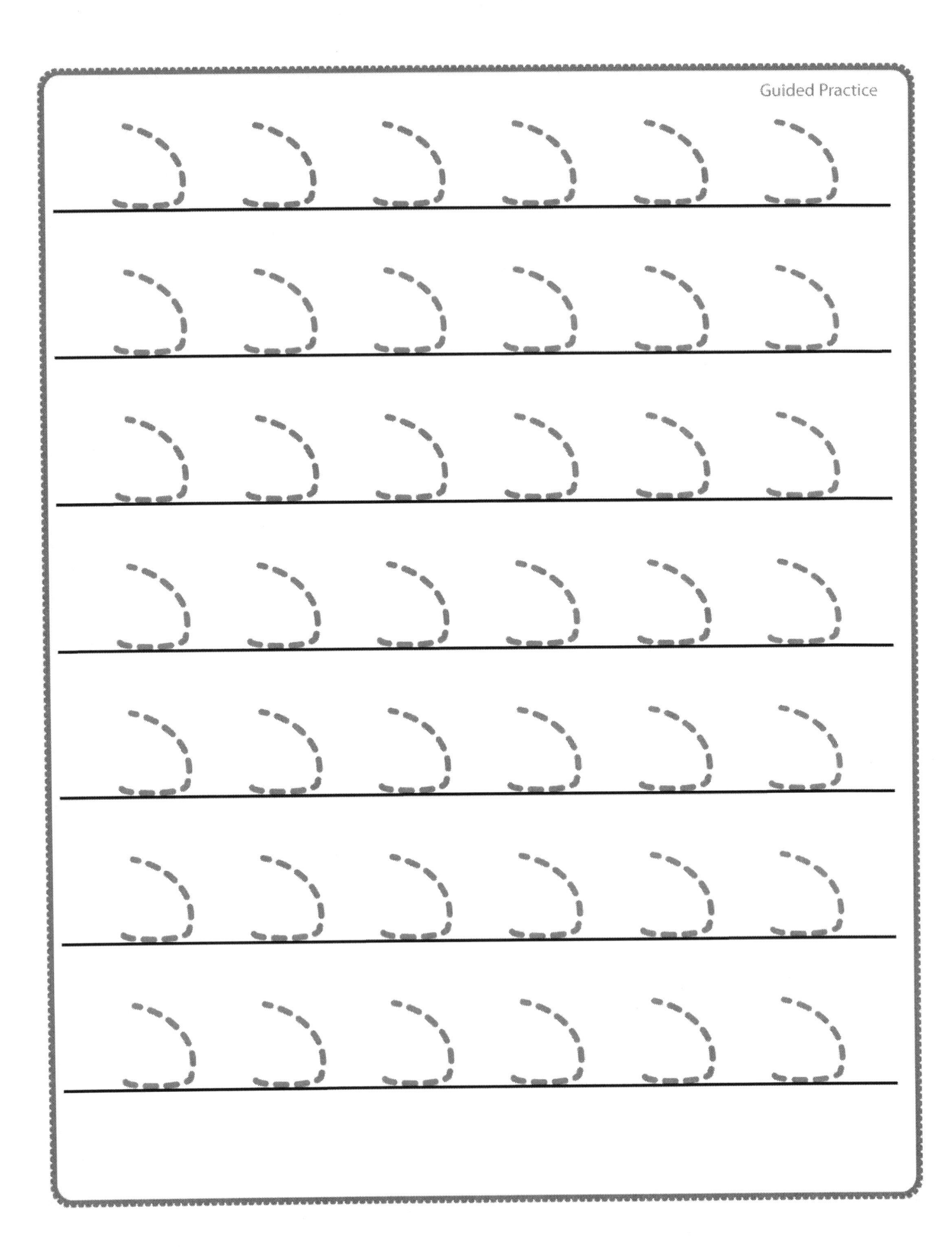

Guided Practice

Guided Practice

Guided Practice

Lesson: 9

How to write it:
Begin at the top of the letter. Follow the arrow down to the right and across the bottom ending on the left. Finish with one dot above the letter.

Dhaal (dh)

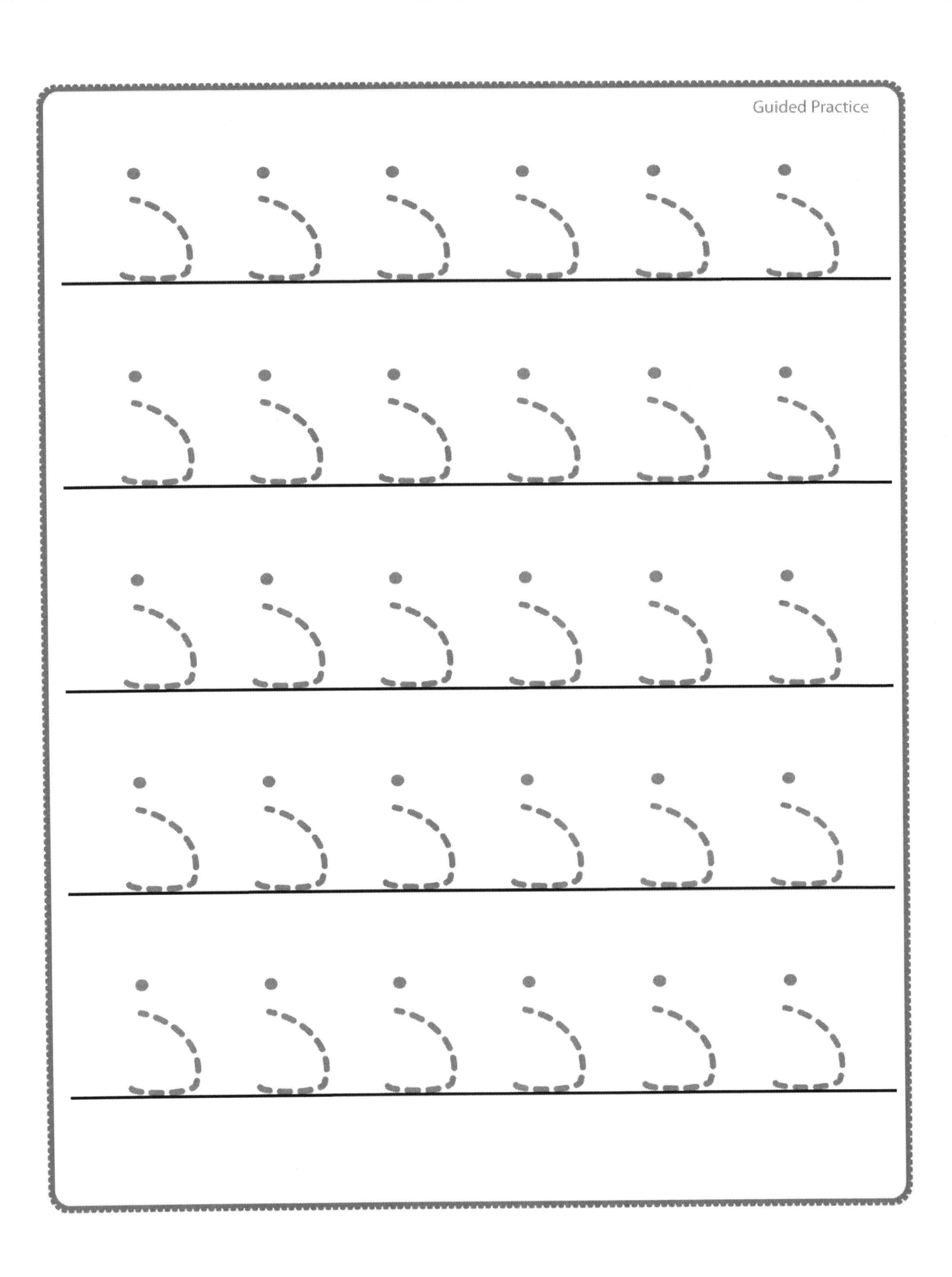

Guided Practice

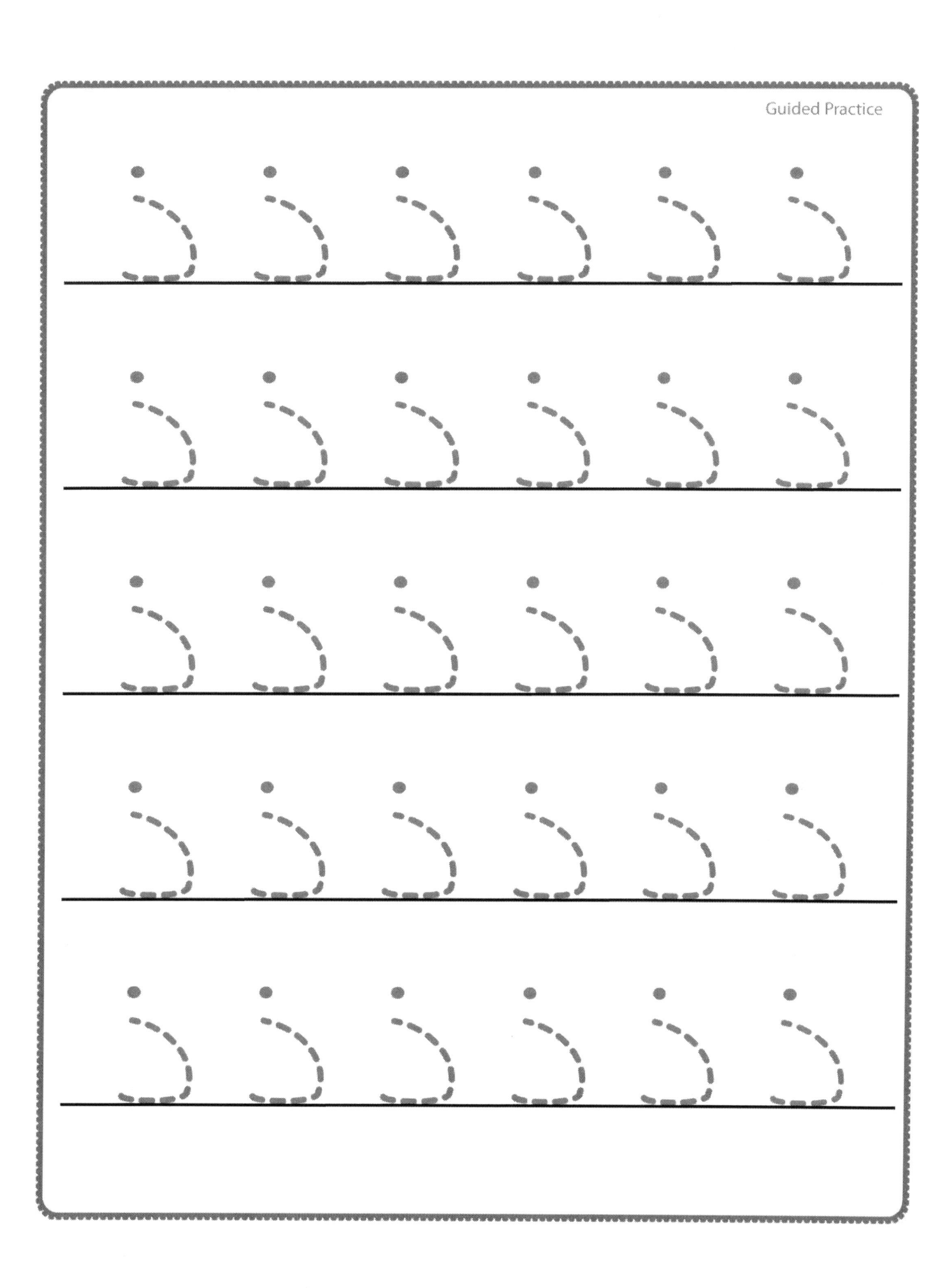

Guided Practice

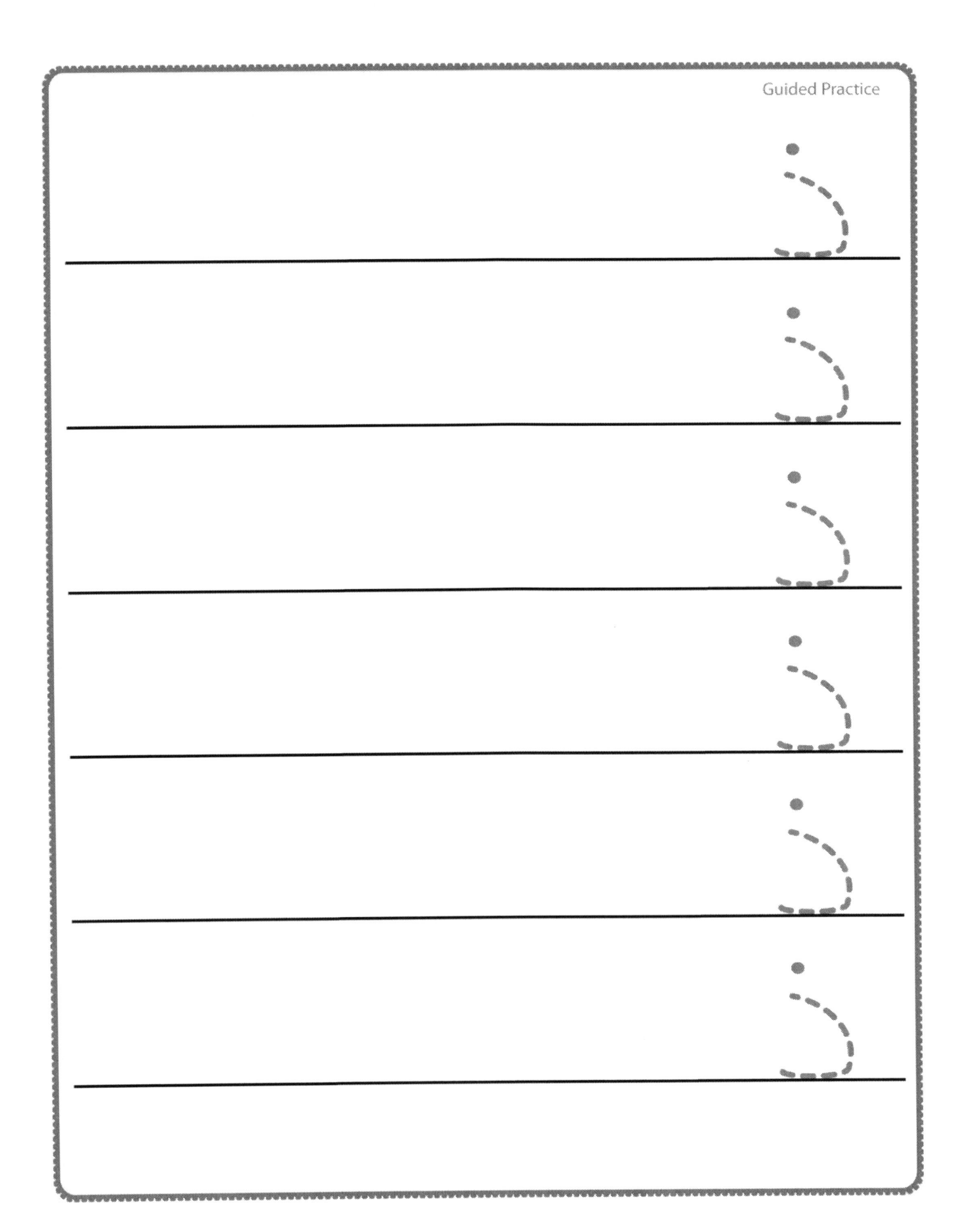

Guided Practice

Guided Practice

j

j

j

j

j

j

Lesson: 10

How to write it:
Begin at the top of the letter. Follow the arrows down and around in a curve ending on the left.

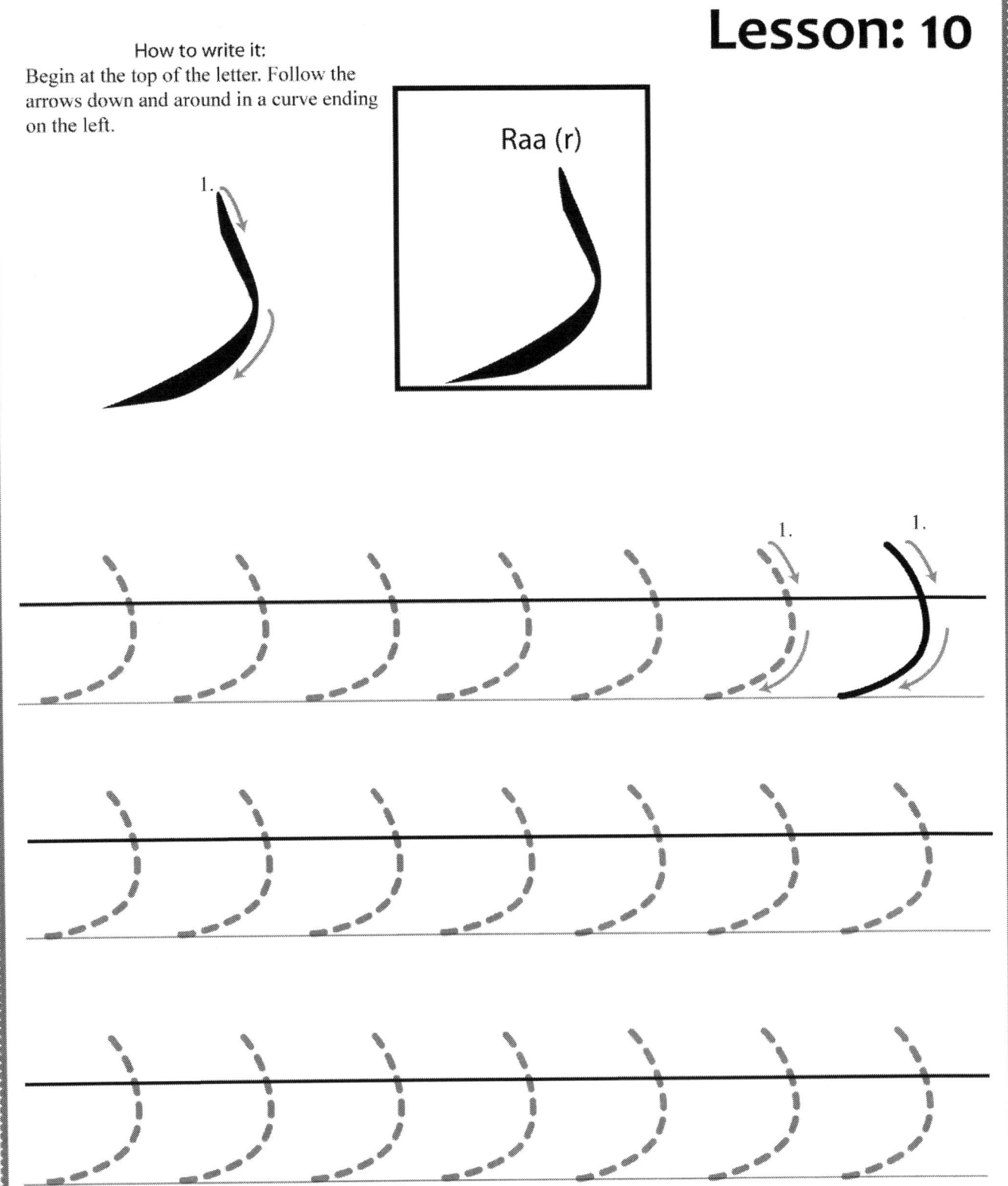

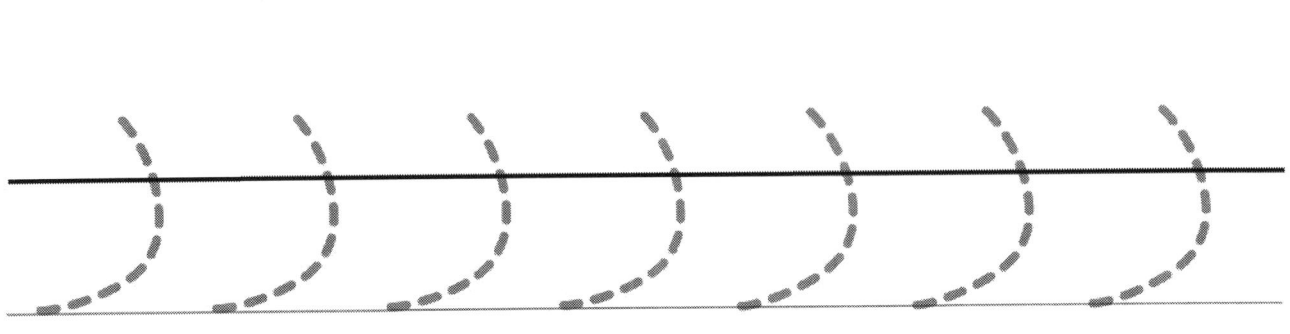

Raa (r)

Guided Practice

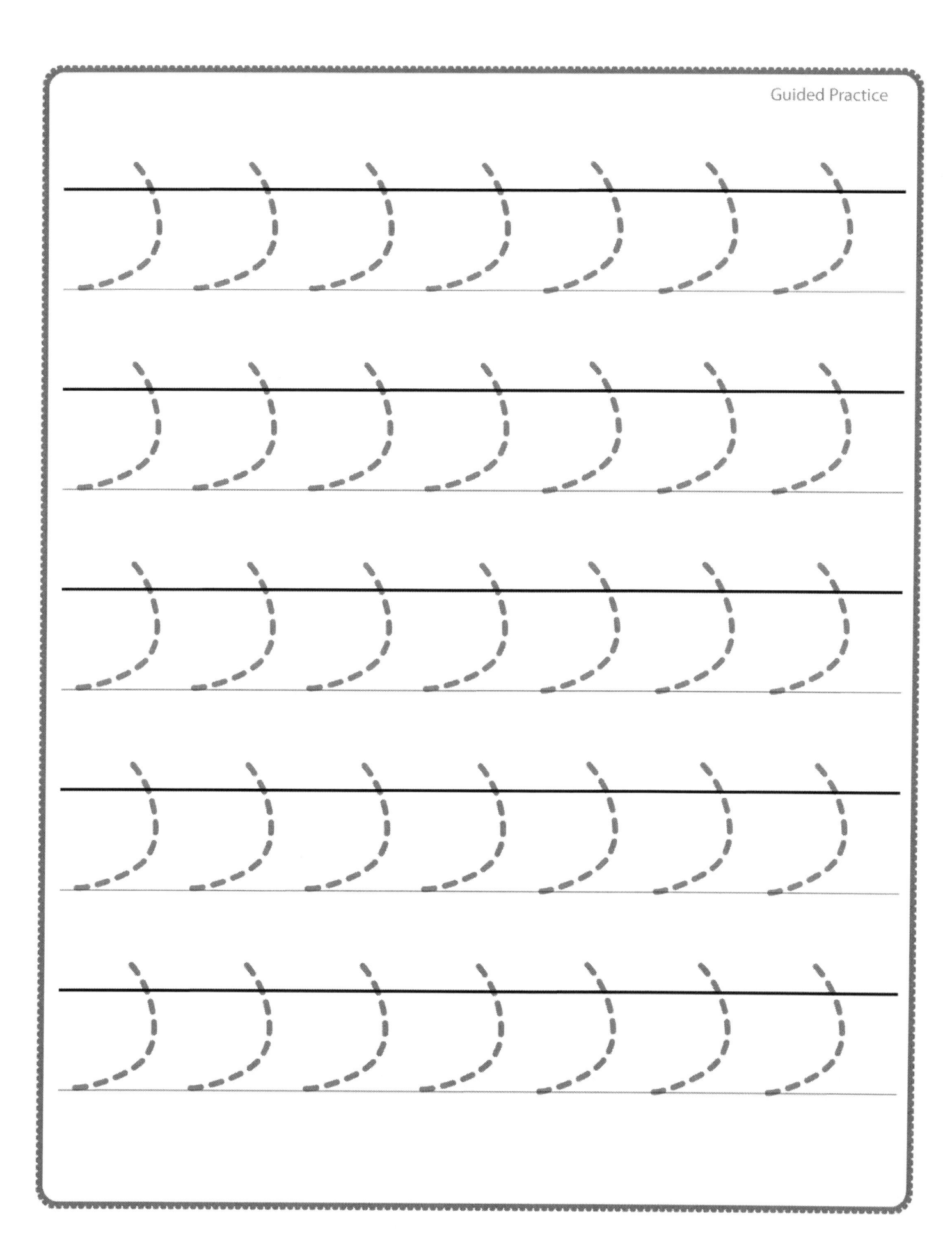

Guided Practice

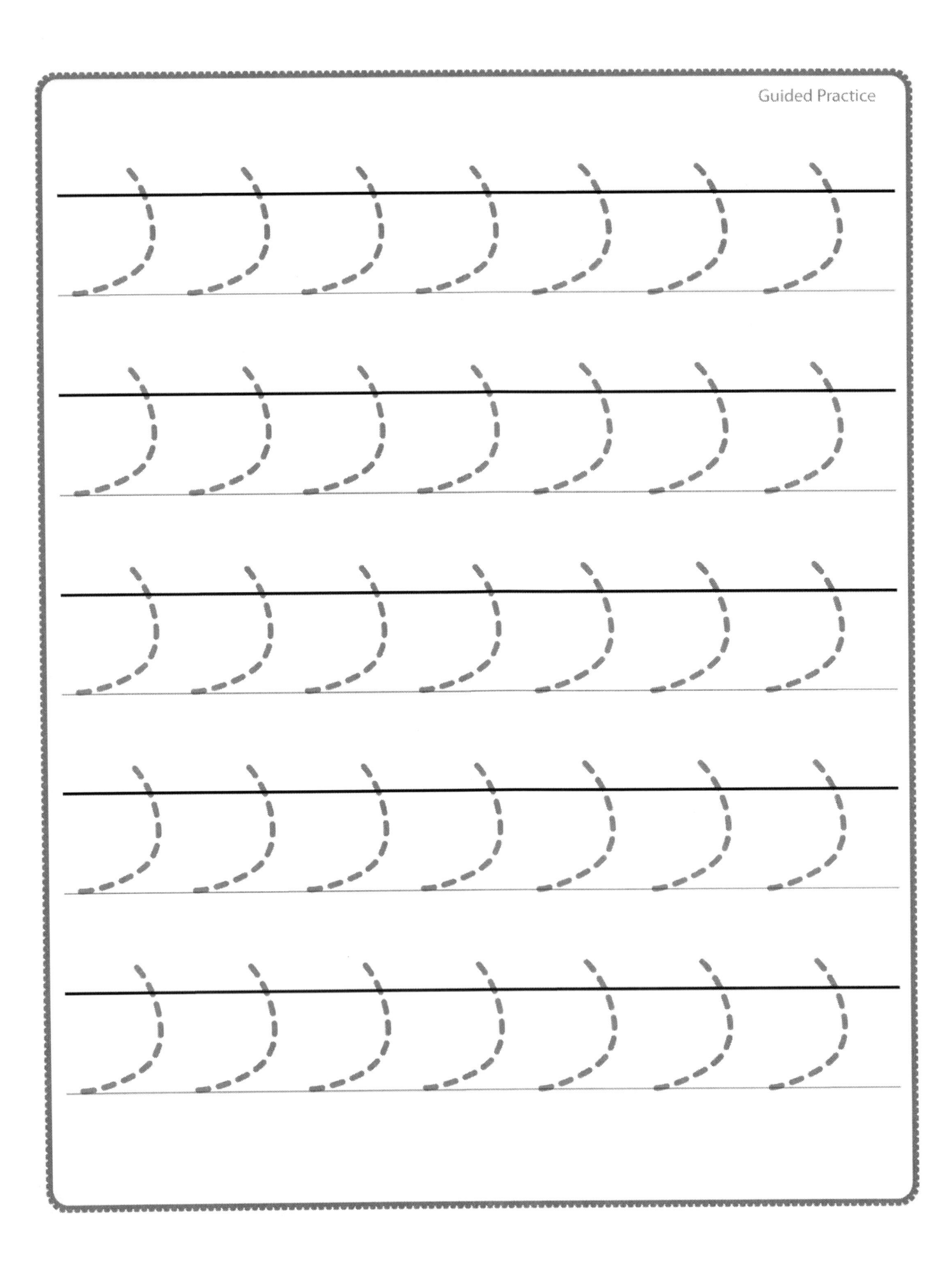

Guided Practice

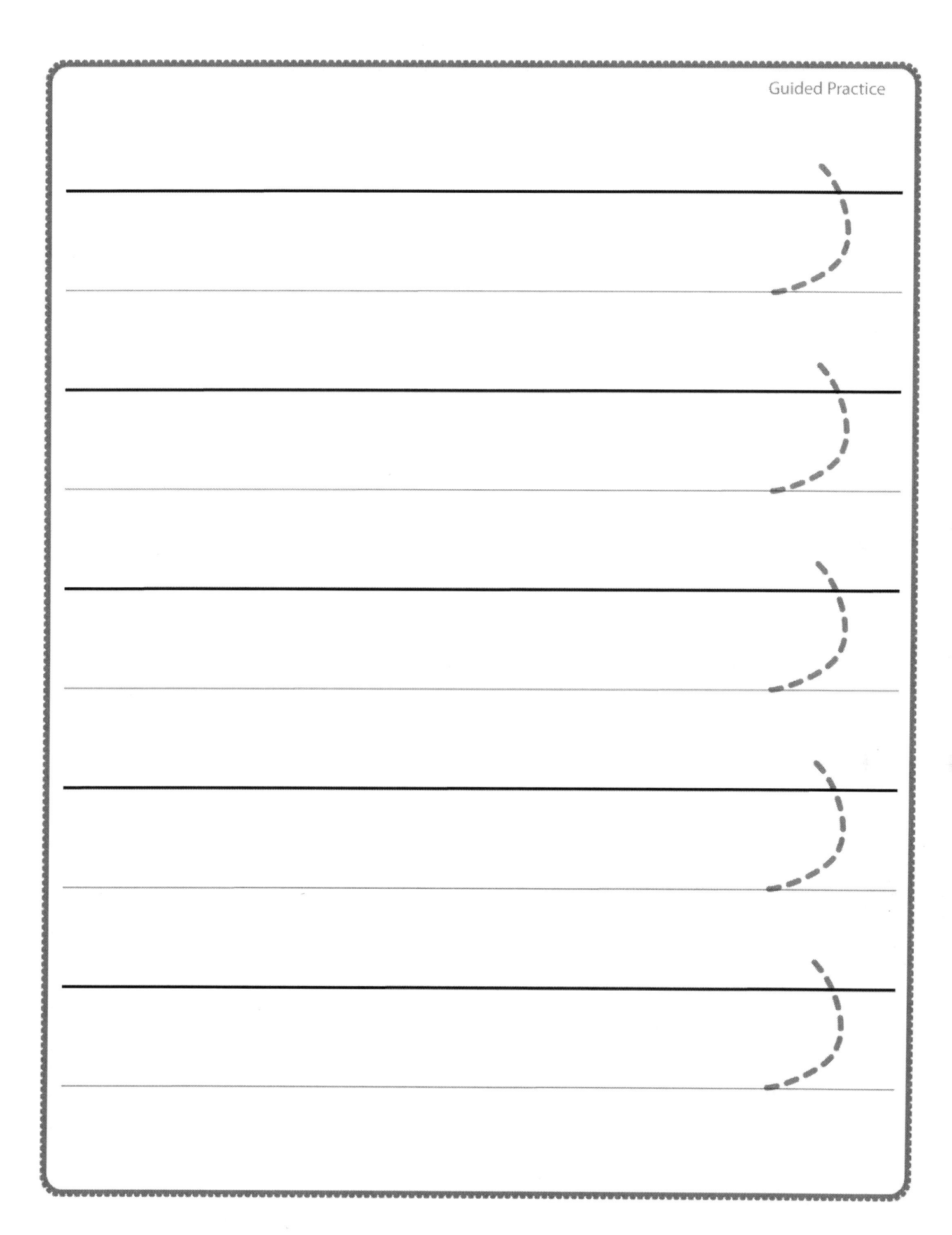

Guided Practice

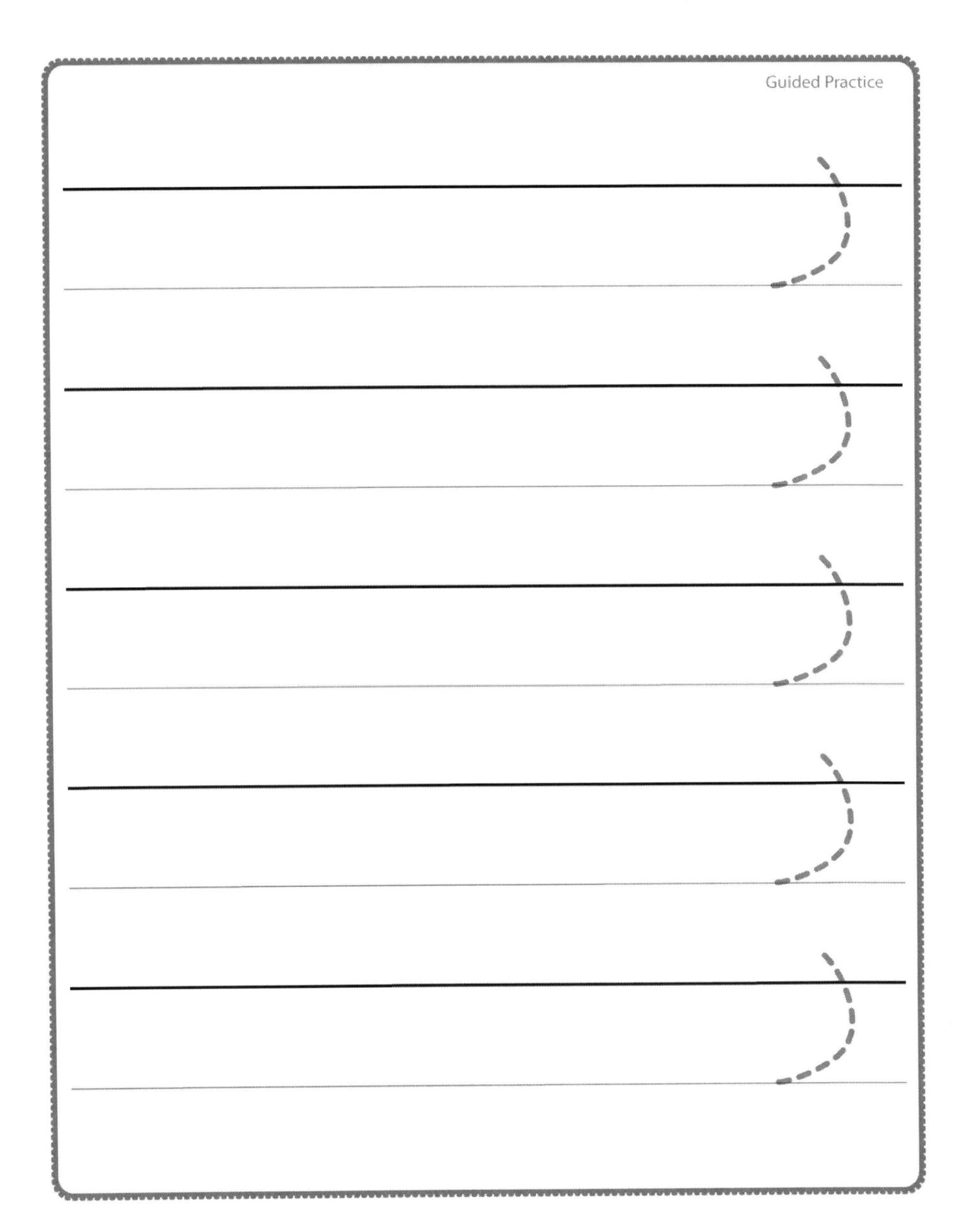

Lesson: 11

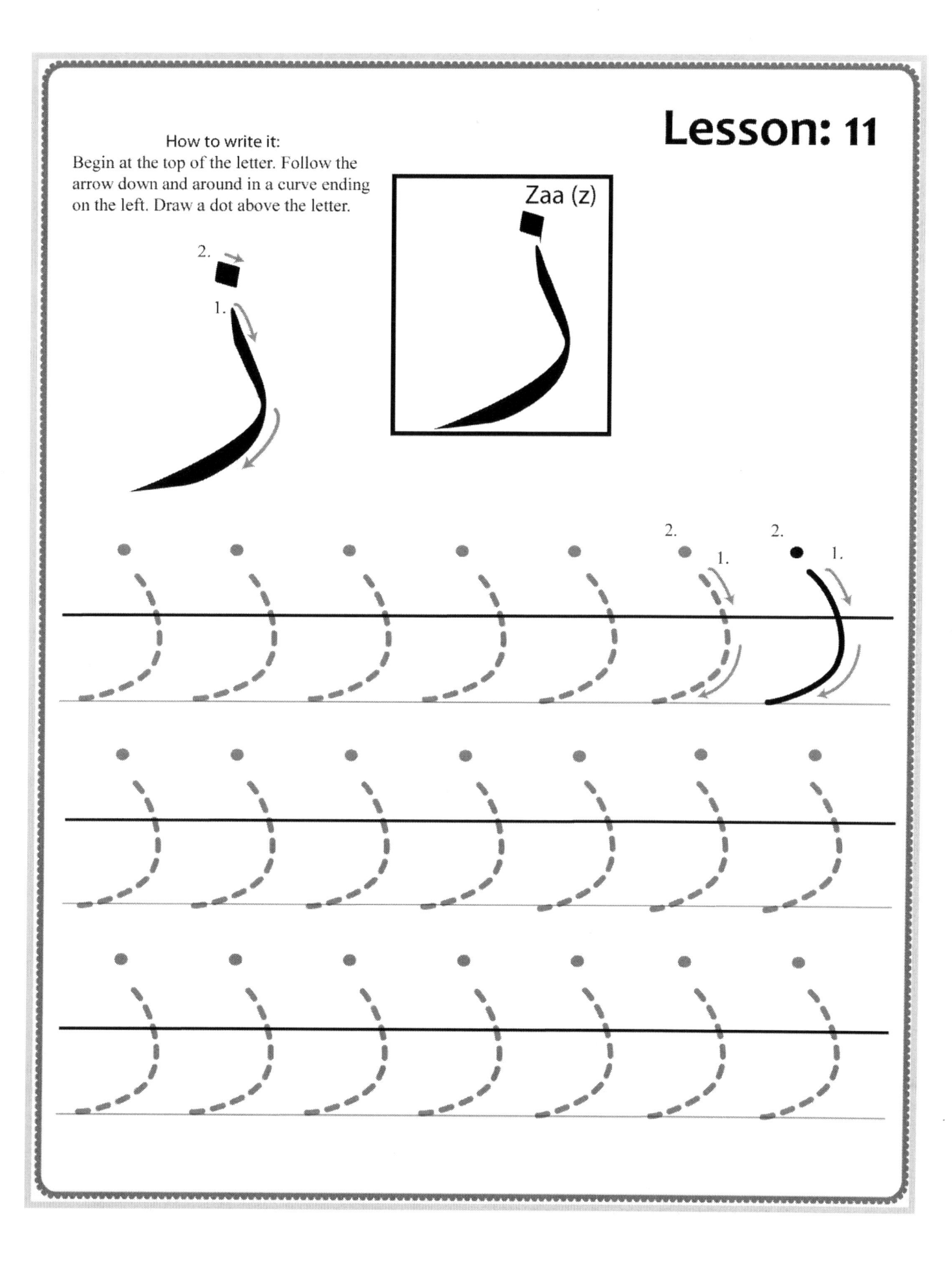

How to write it:
Begin at the top of the letter. Follow the arrow down and around in a curve ending on the left. Draw a dot above the letter.

Zaa (z)

Guided Practice

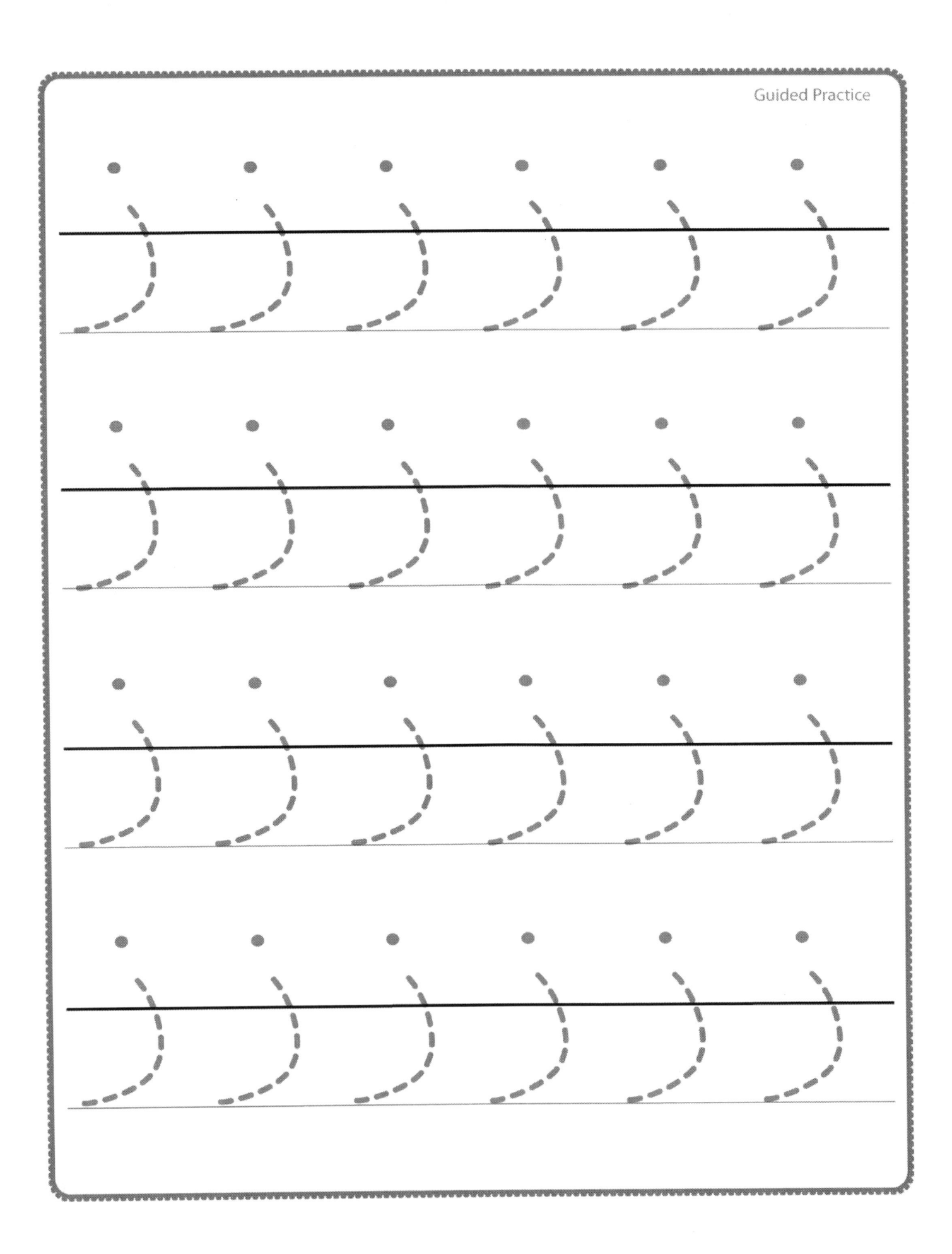

Guided Practice

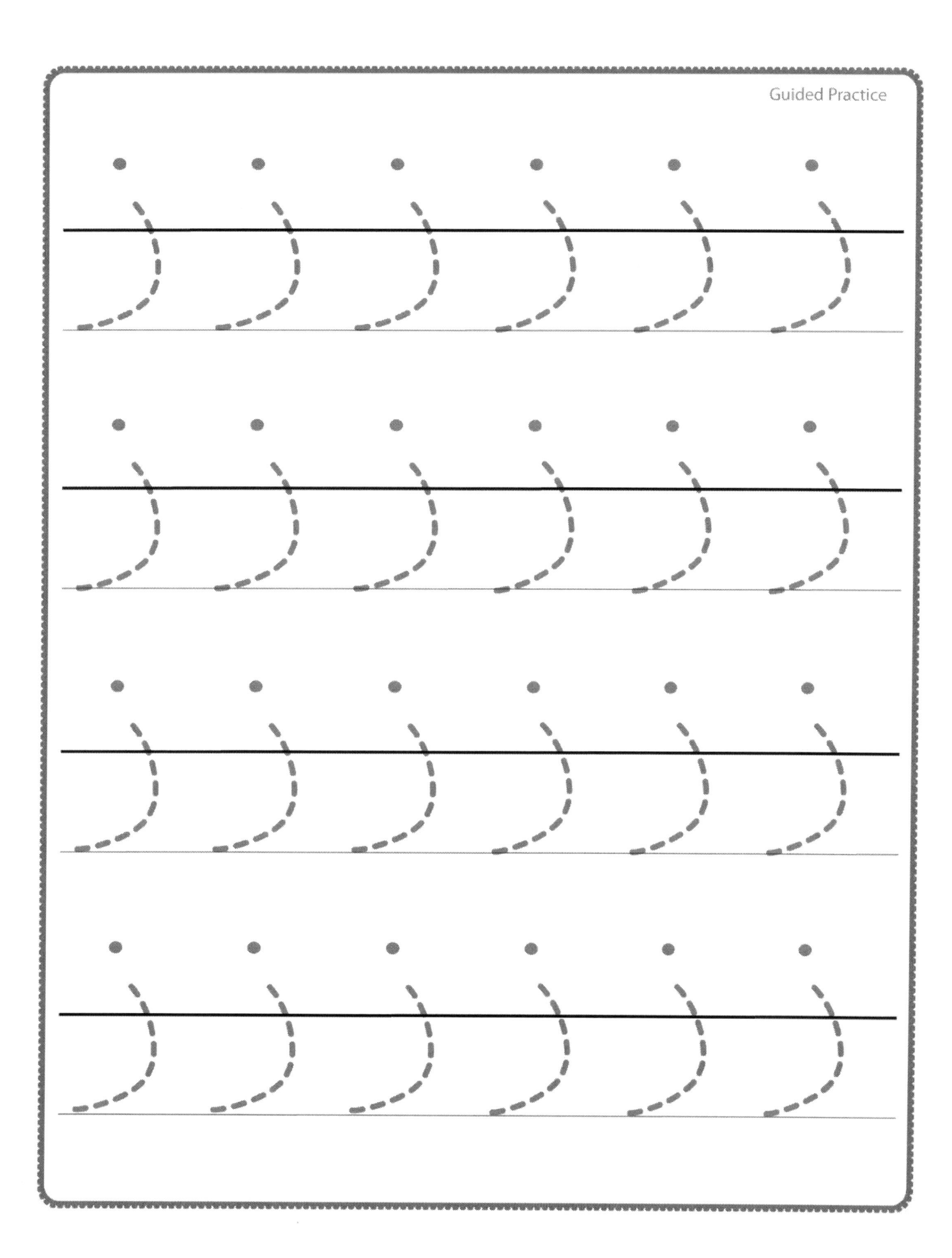

Guided Practice

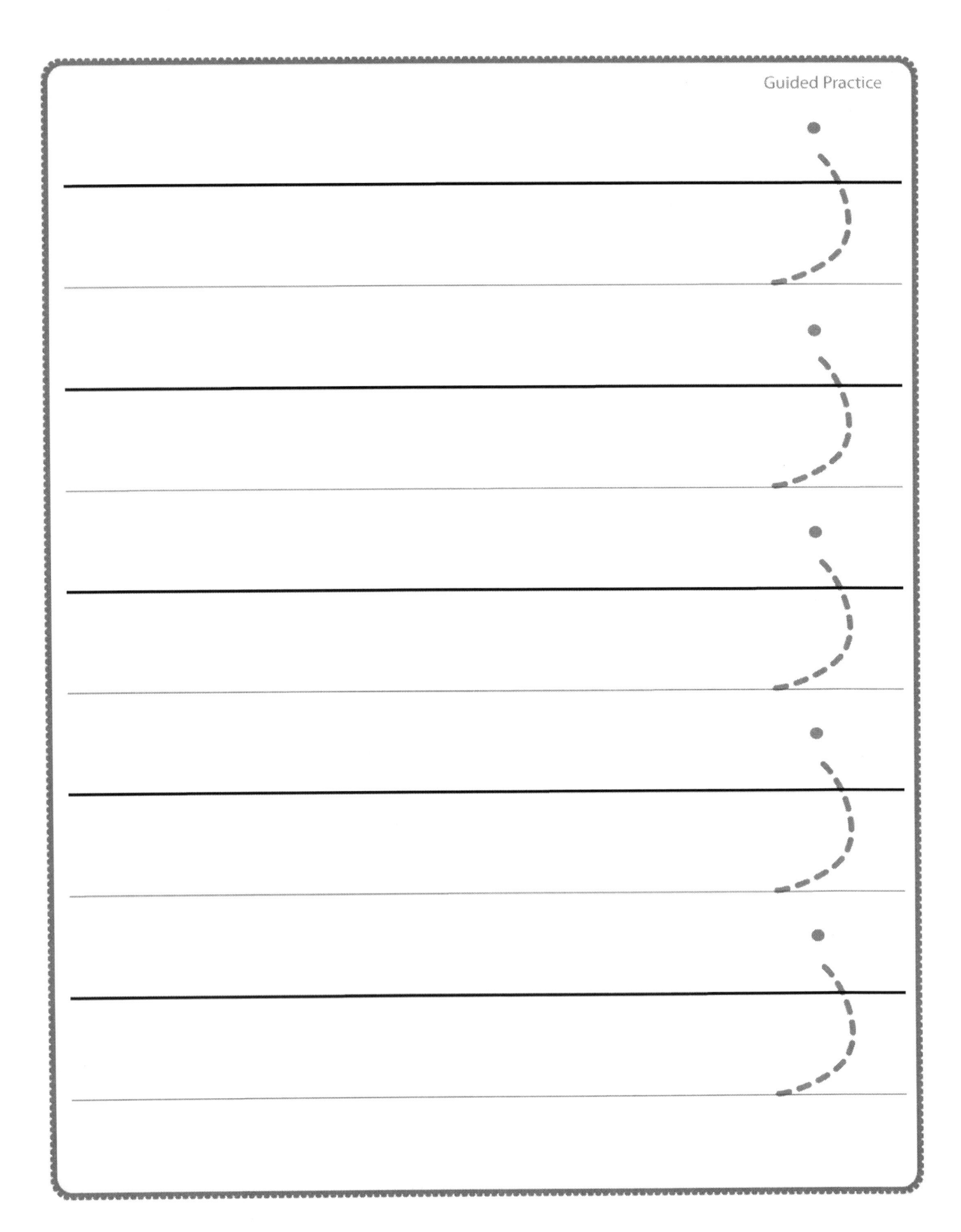

Guided Practice

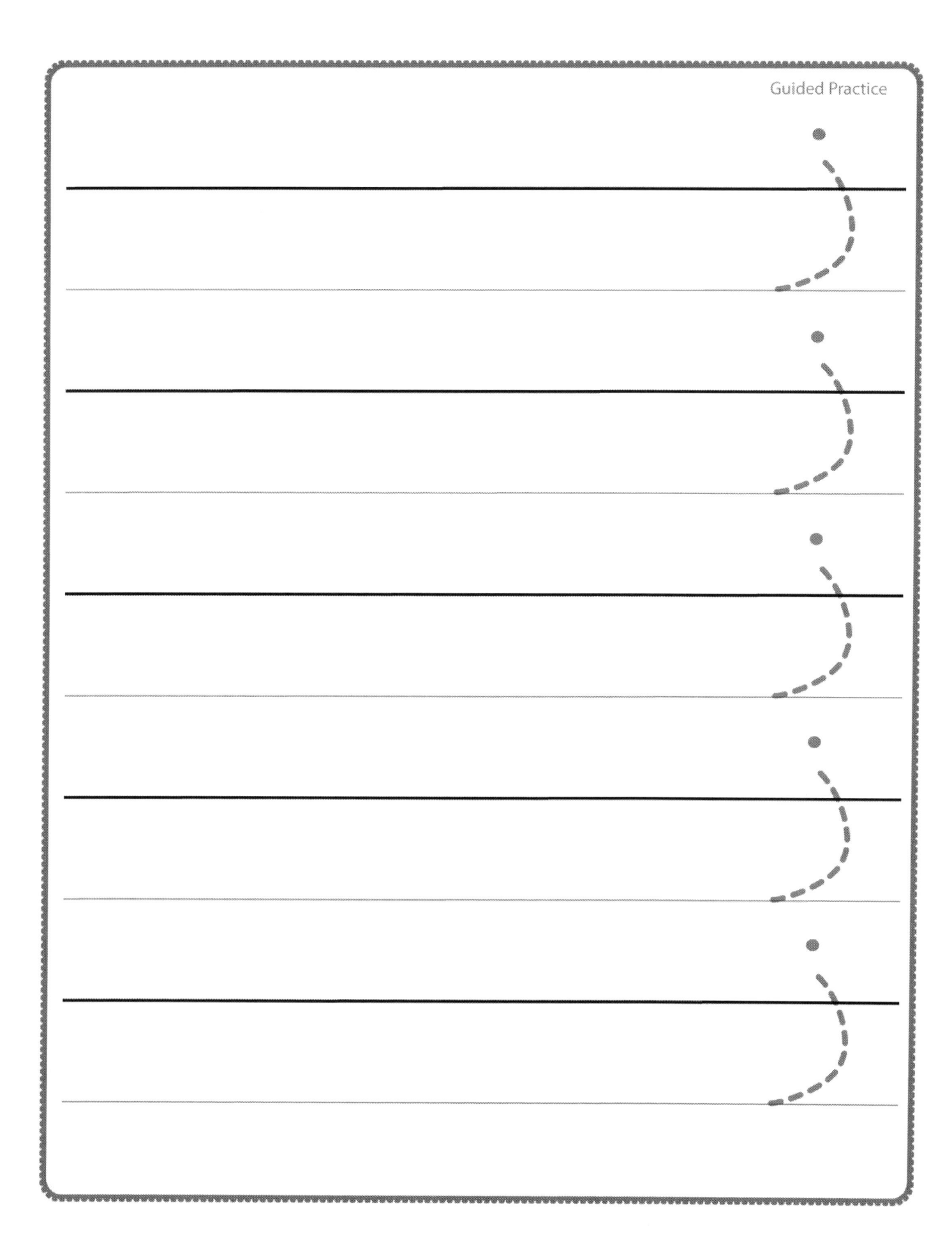

Lesson: 12

How to write it:
The head of this letter rests on the line. Begin from the right with a u-shaped curve, repeat this movement and then follow the arrow as it swoops under the line in a wider curve.

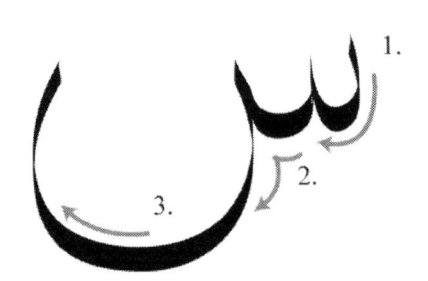

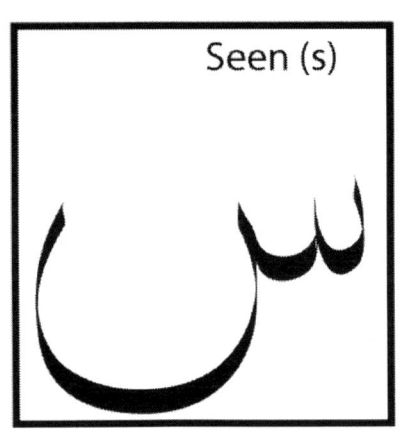

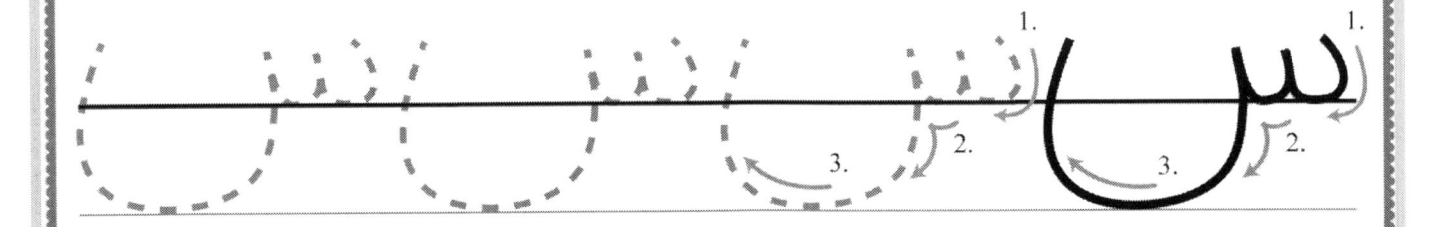

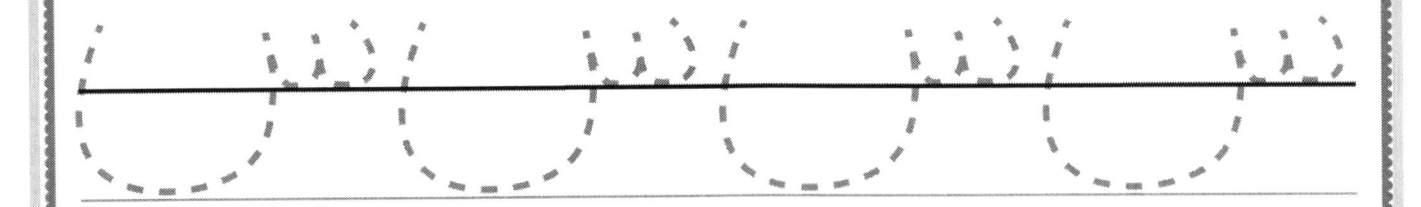

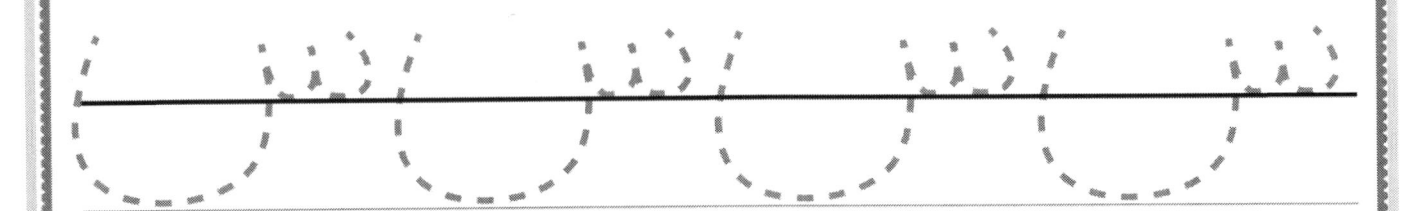

Seen (s)

س

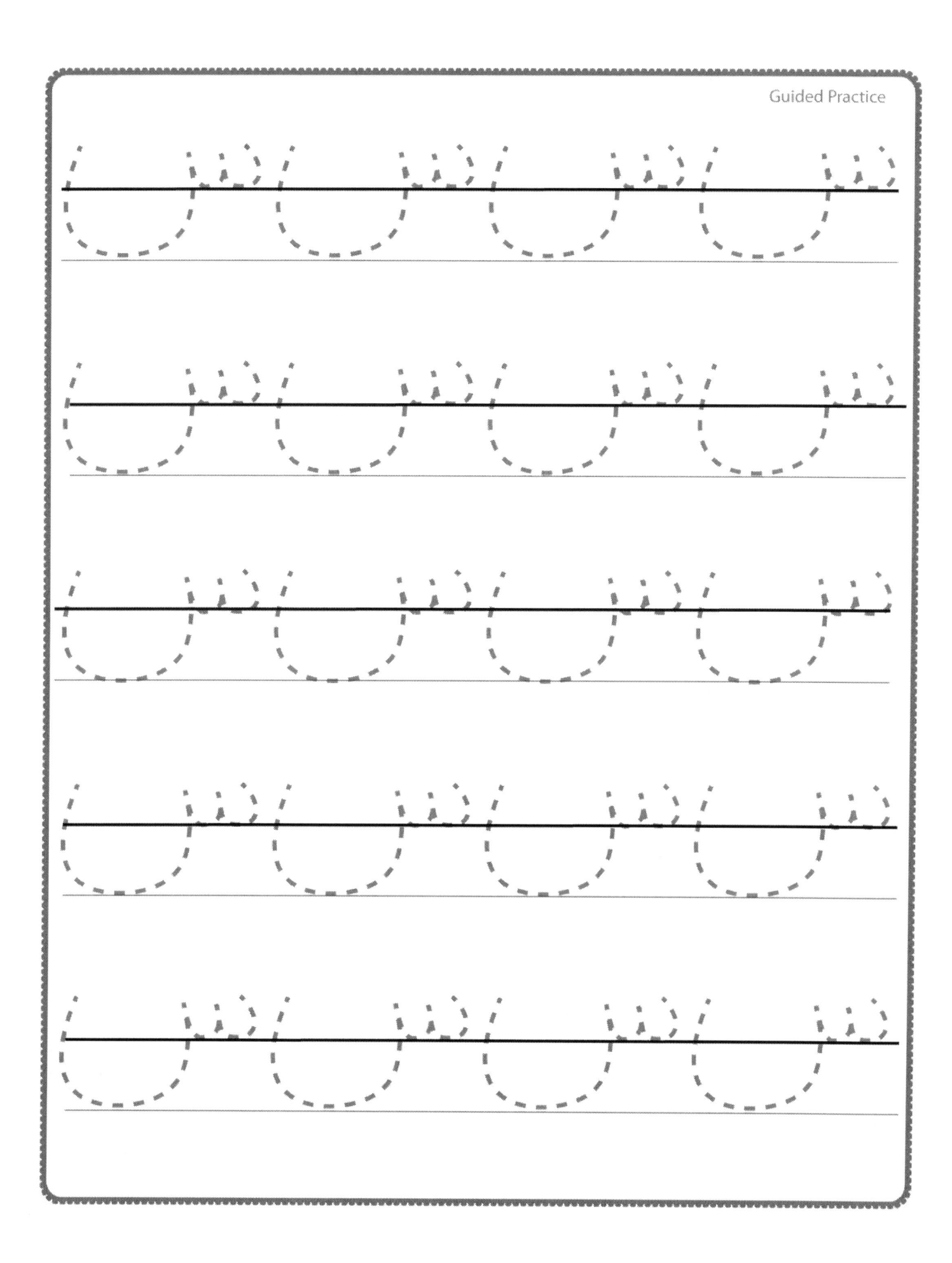

Guided Practice

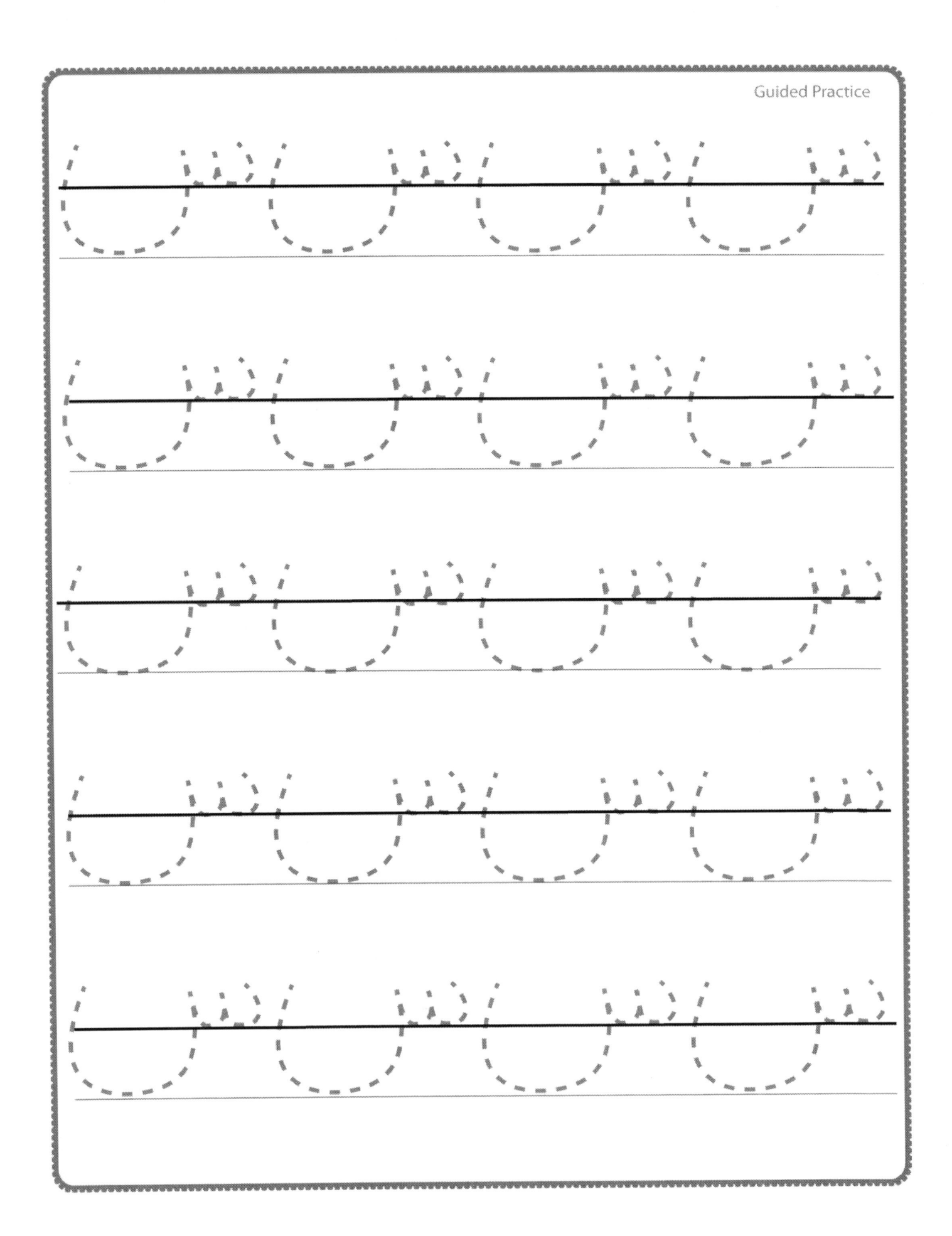

Guided Practice

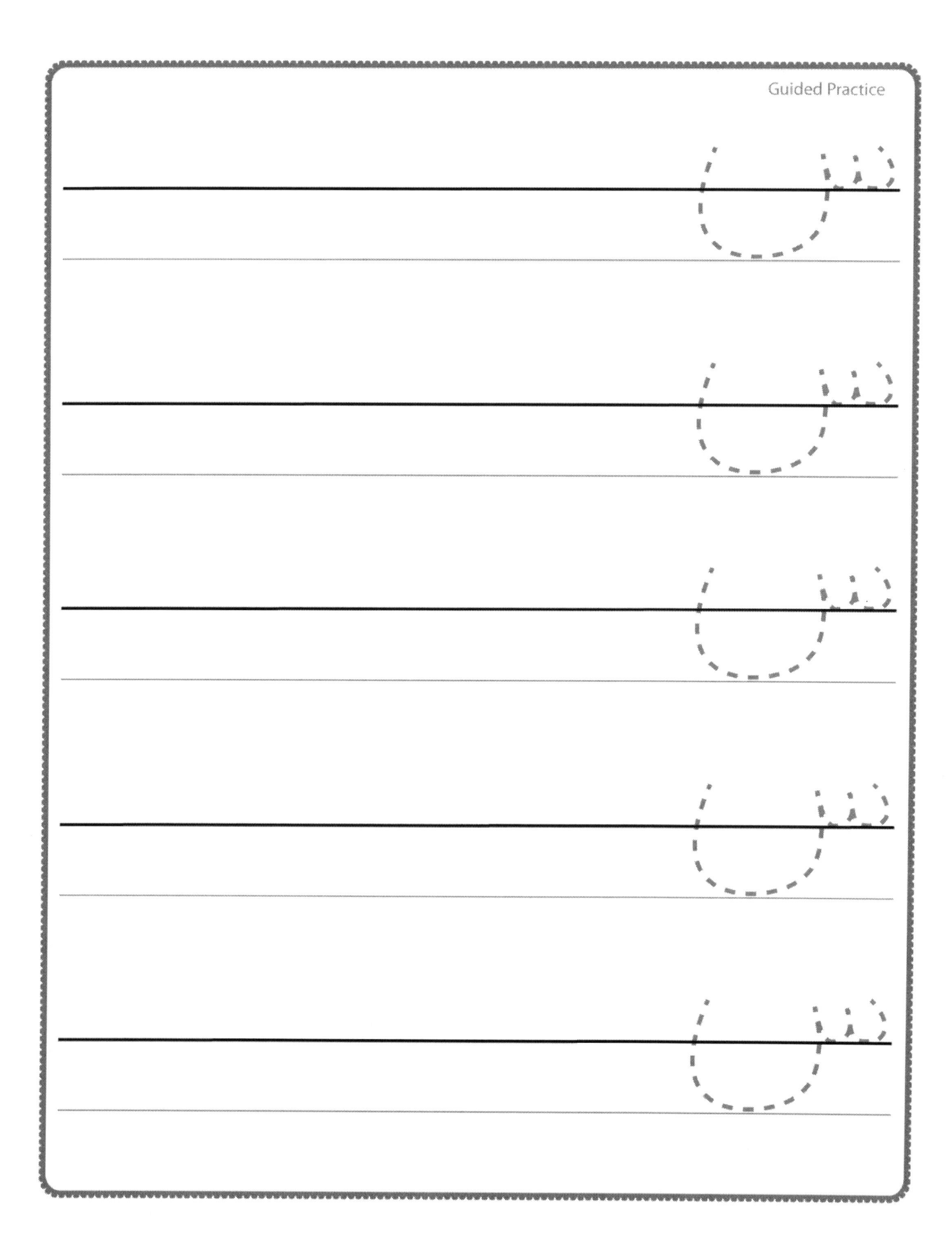

Guided Practice

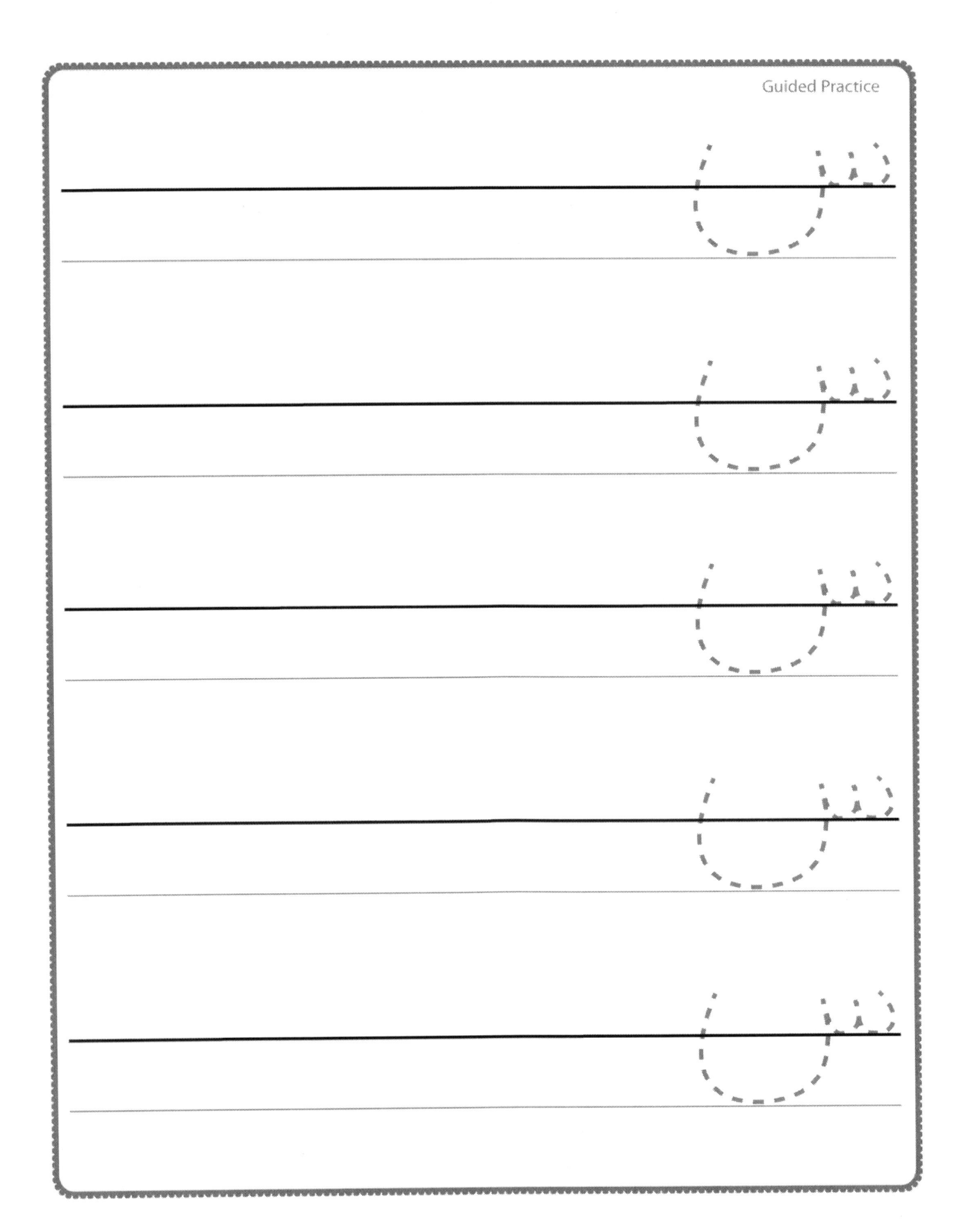

Guided Practice

Lesson: 13

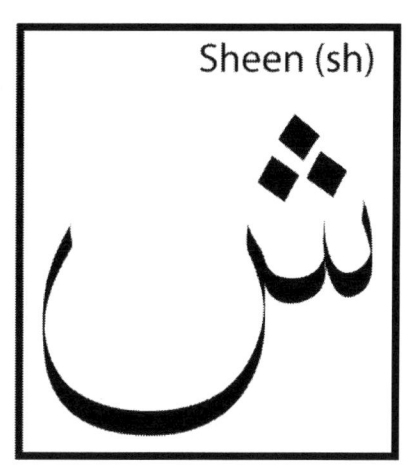

How to write it:
The head of this letter rests on the line. Begin from the right with a u-shaped curve, repeat this movement and then follow the arrow as it swoops under the line in a wider curve. Place 3 dots above the letter.

Sheen (sh)

ش

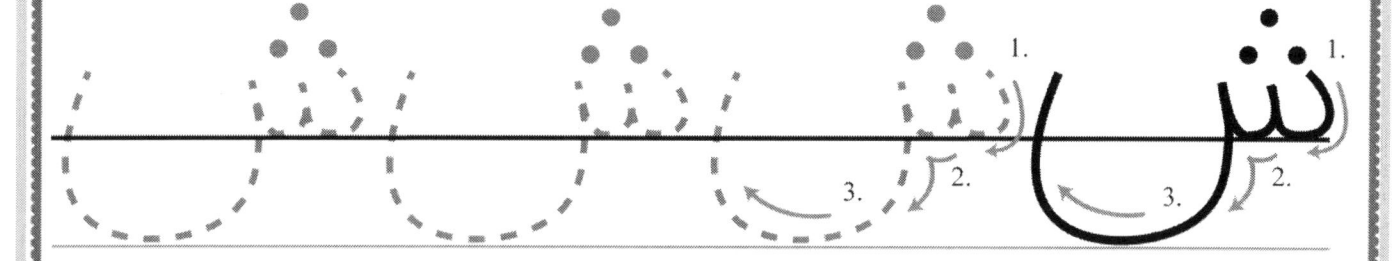

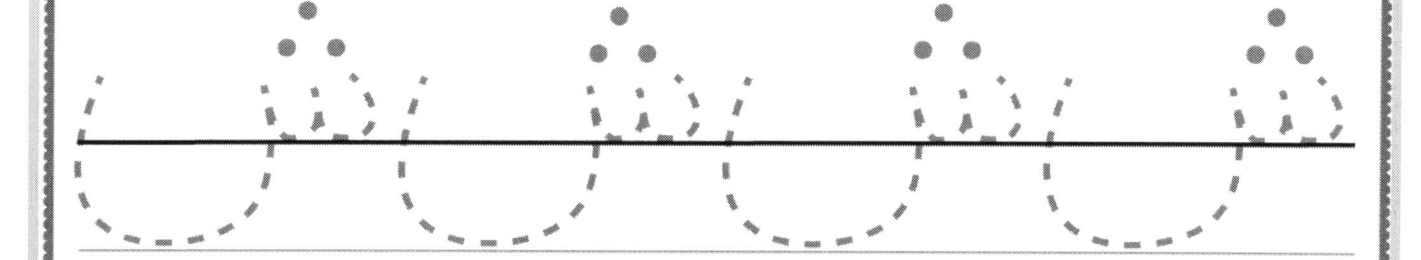

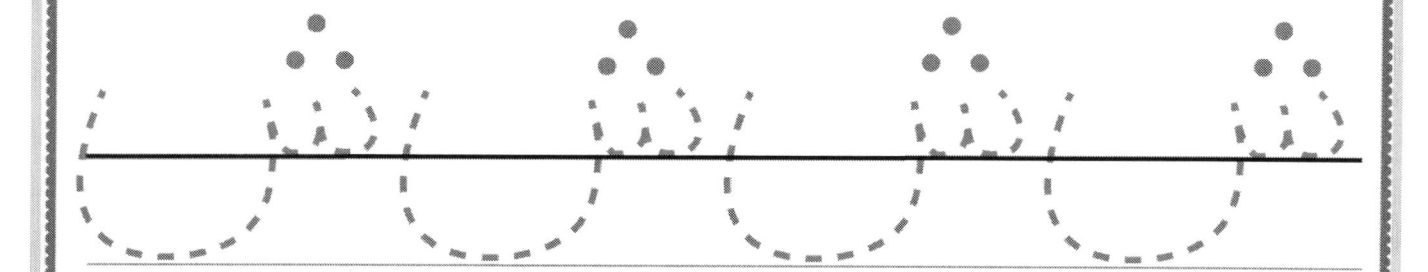

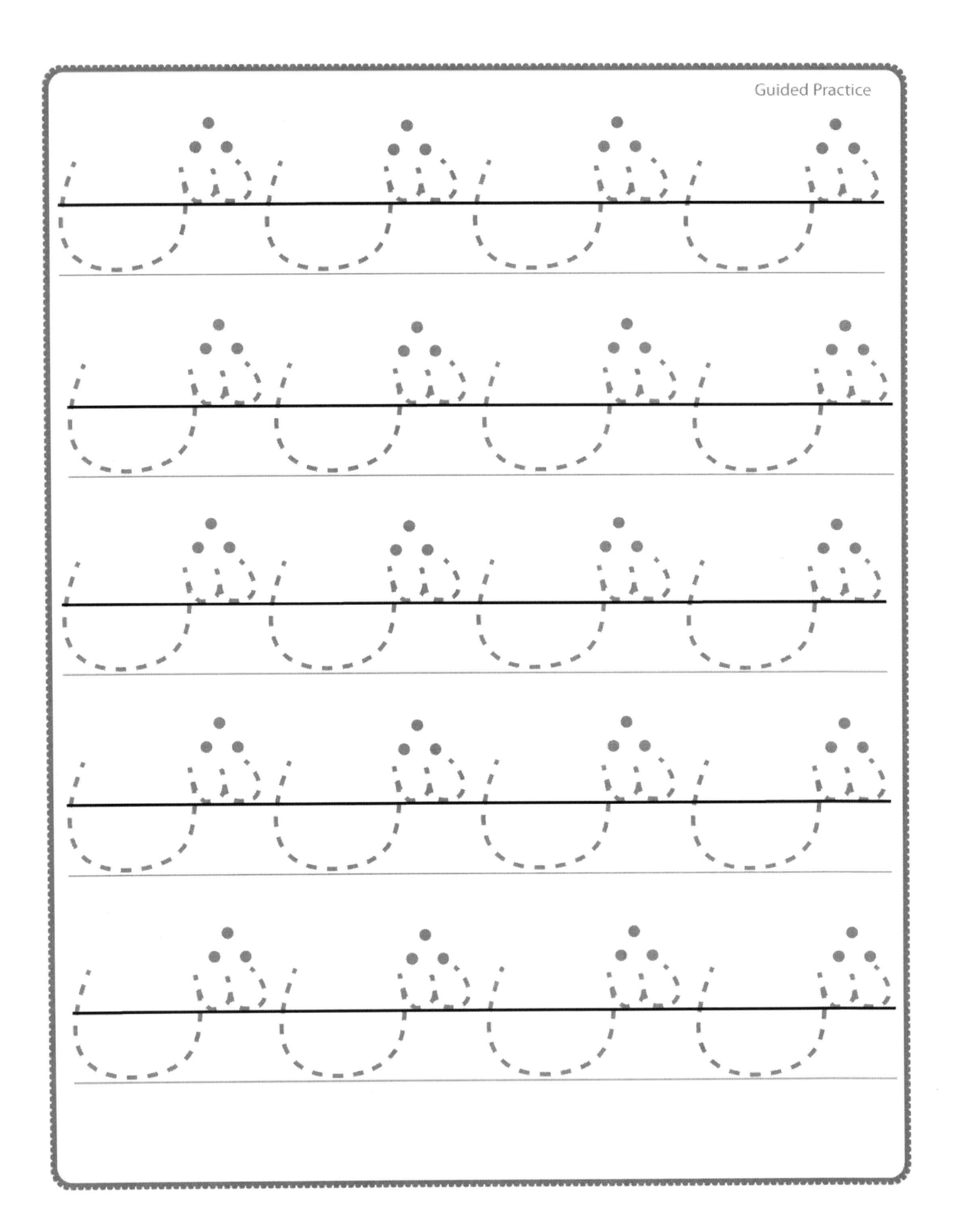

Guided Practice

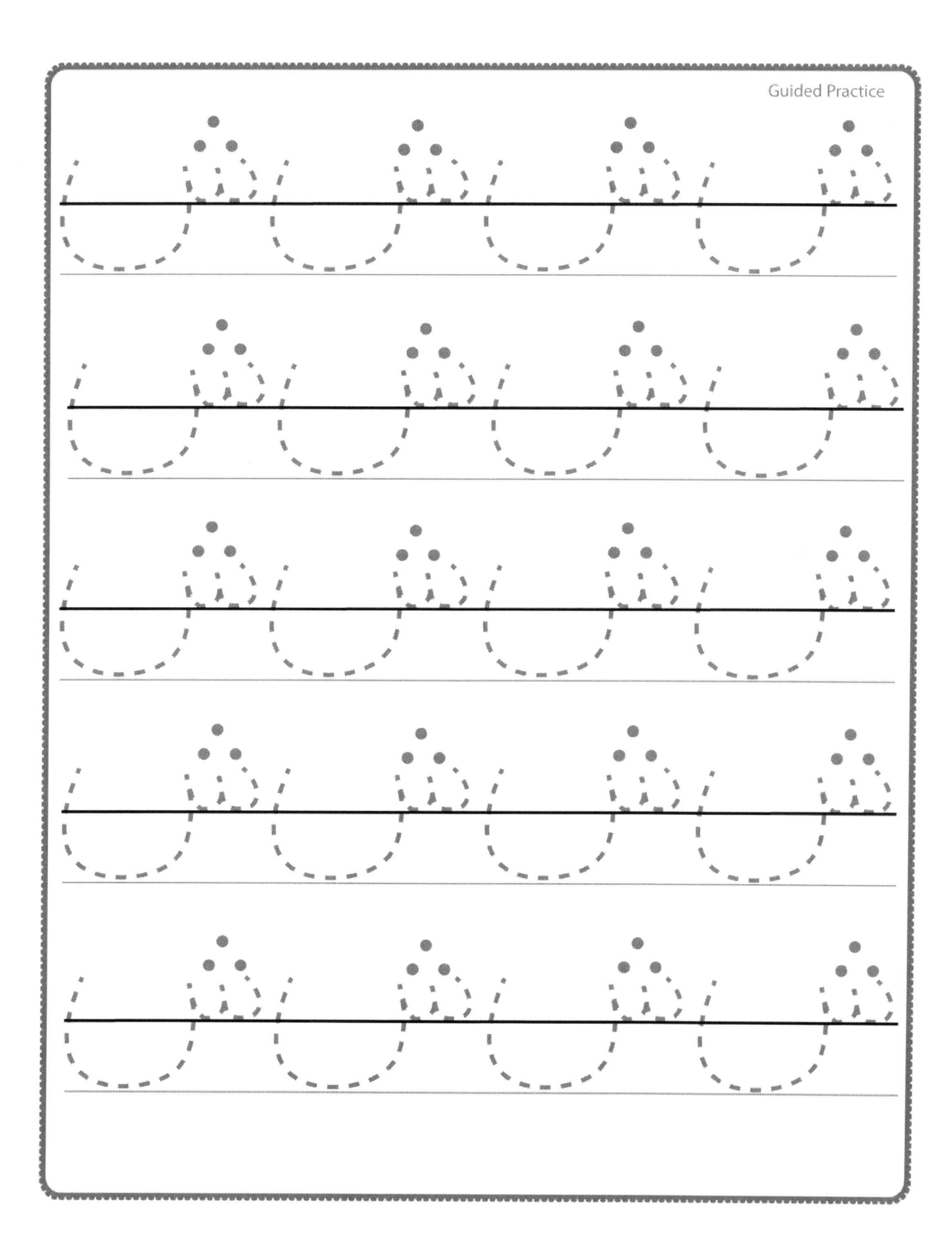

Guided Practice

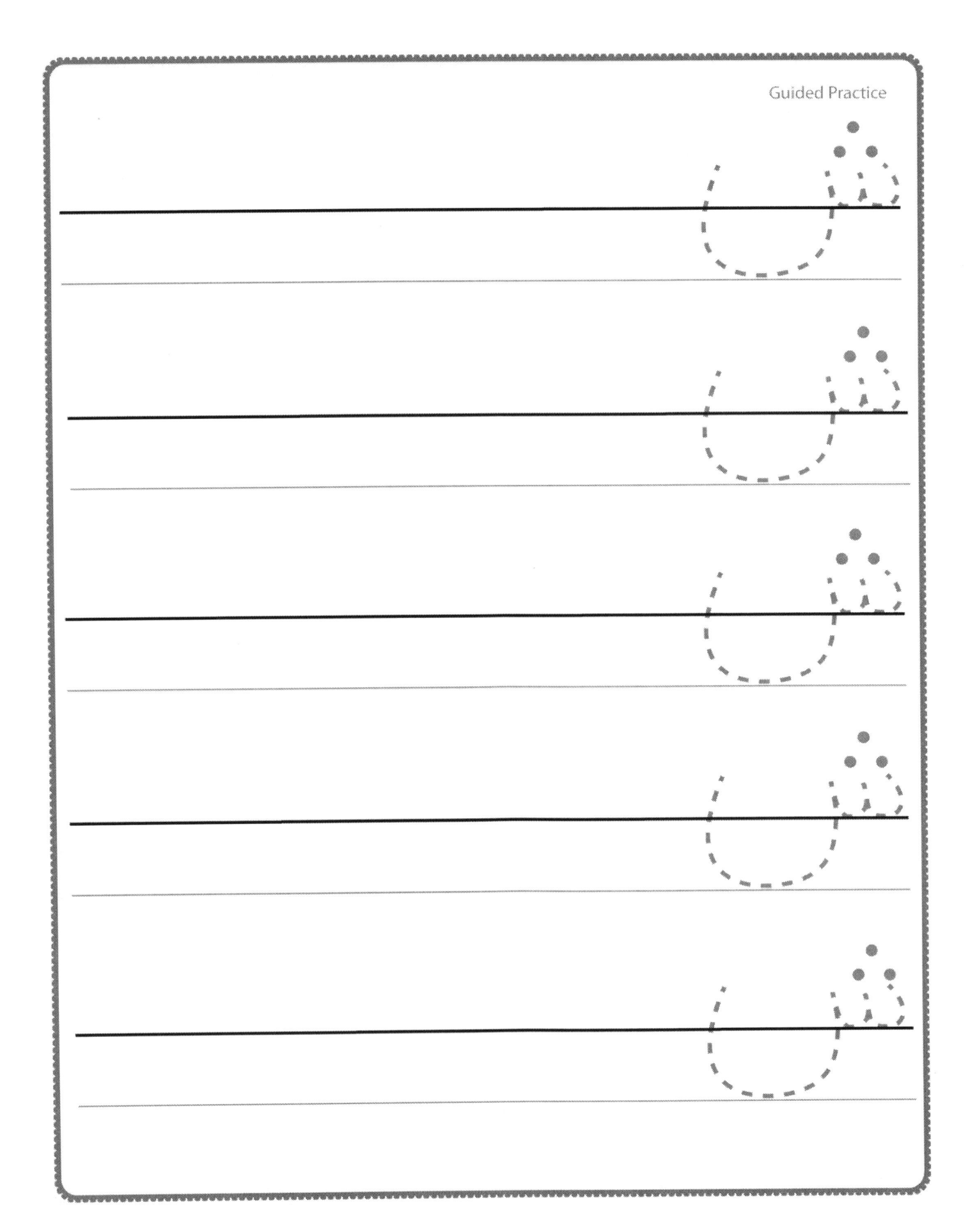

Guided Practice

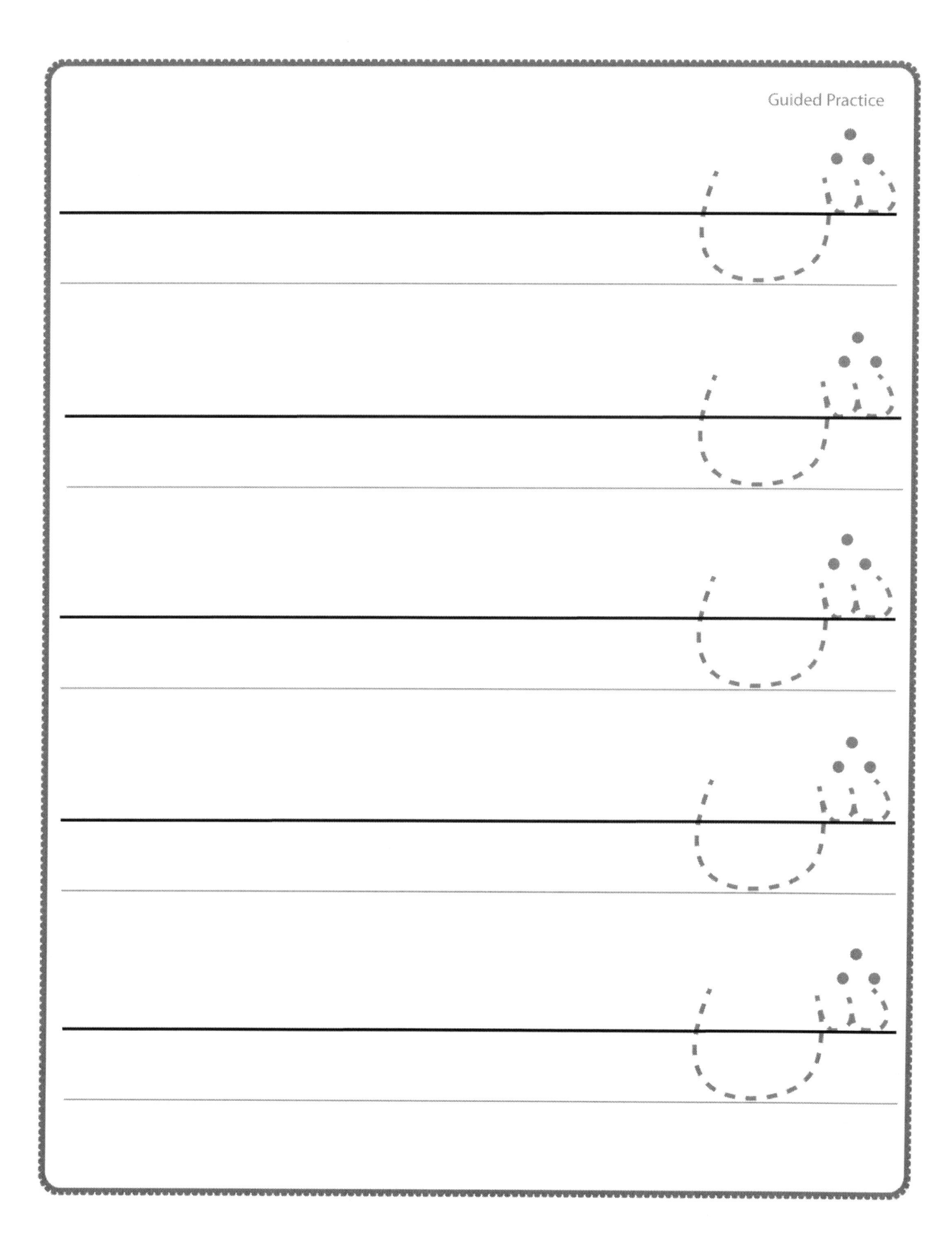

Guided Practice

How to write it:
The head of this letter rests on the line. Begin by drawing a loop, and then follow the arrow as it swoops under the line in a wide curve.

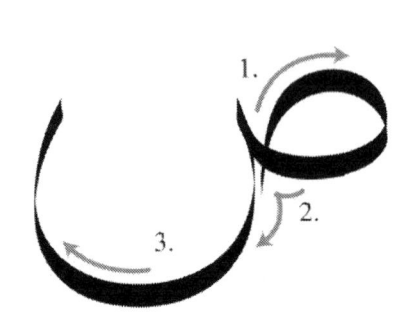

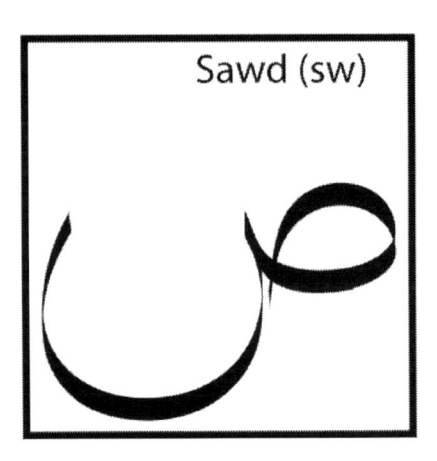

Sawd (sw)

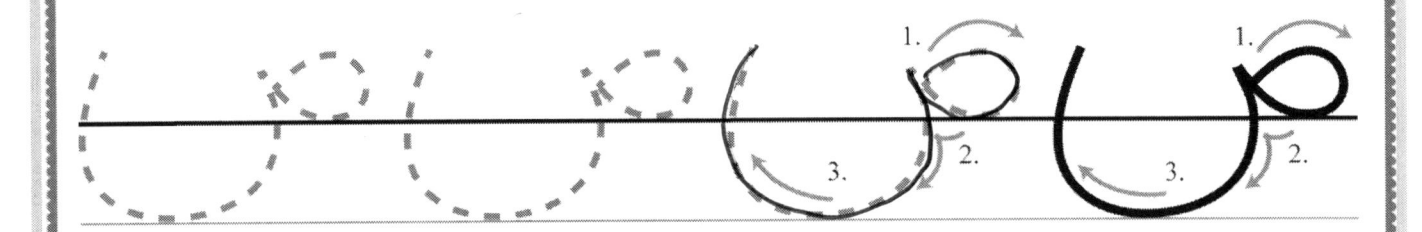

ص

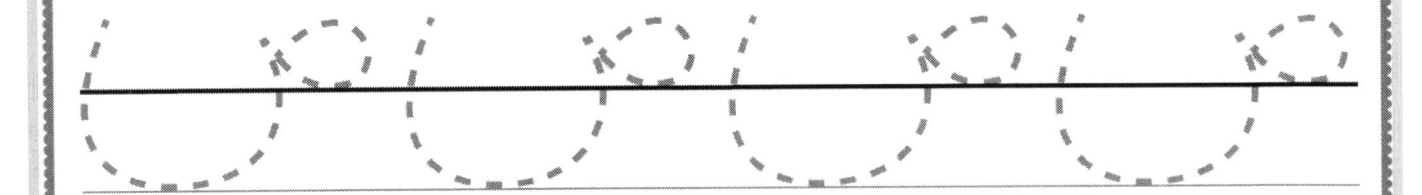

Lesson: 14

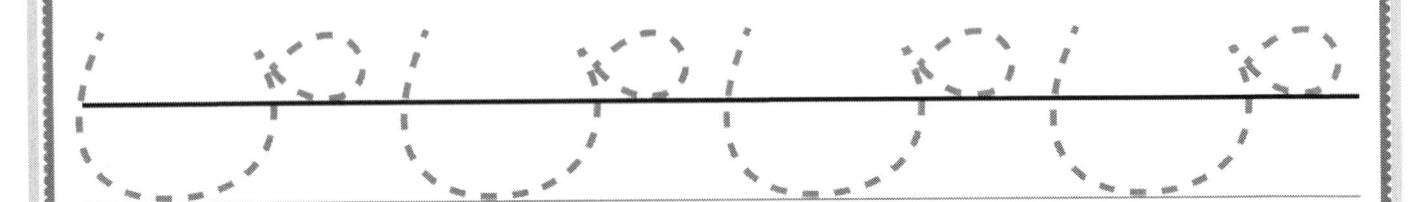

Guided Practice

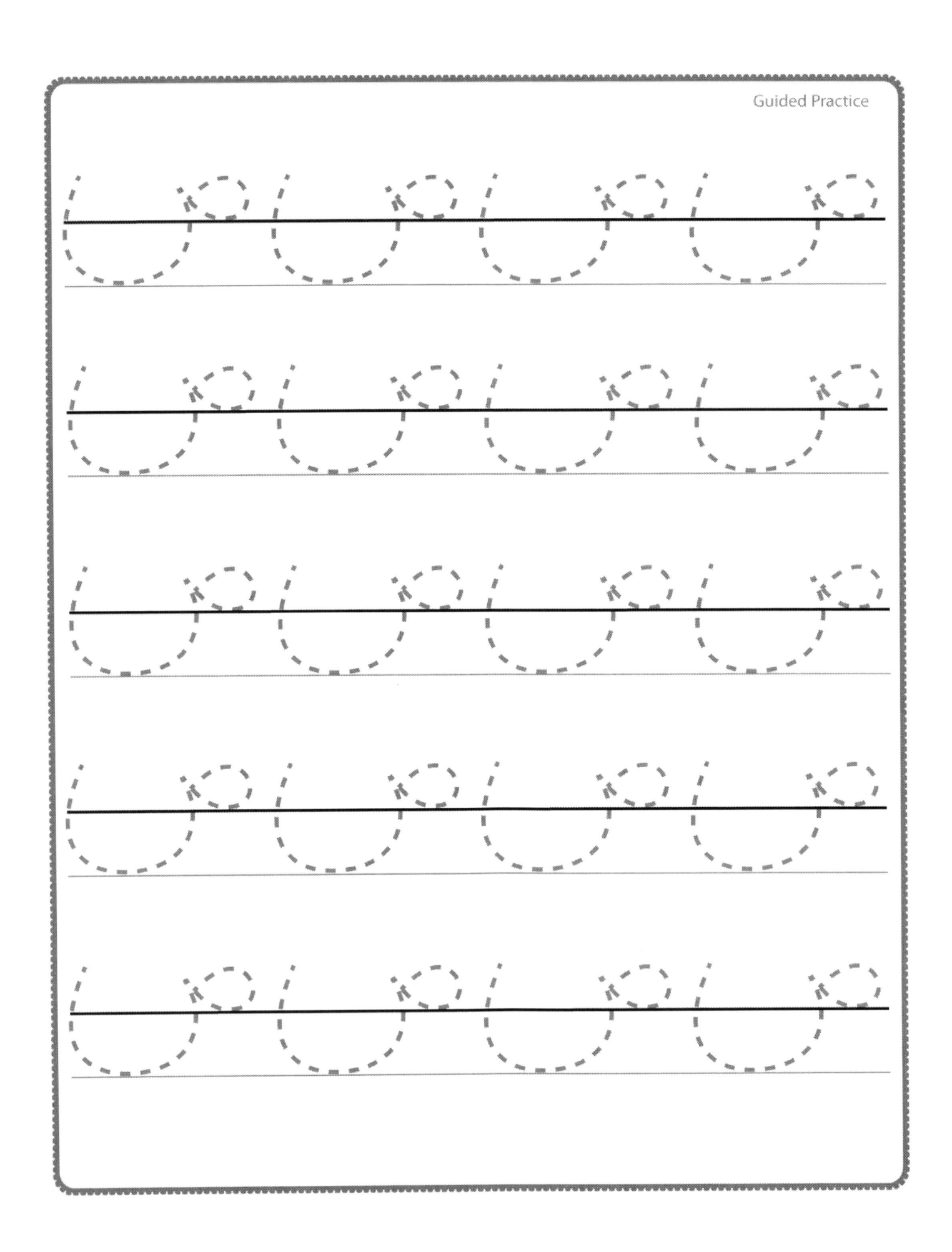

Guided Practice

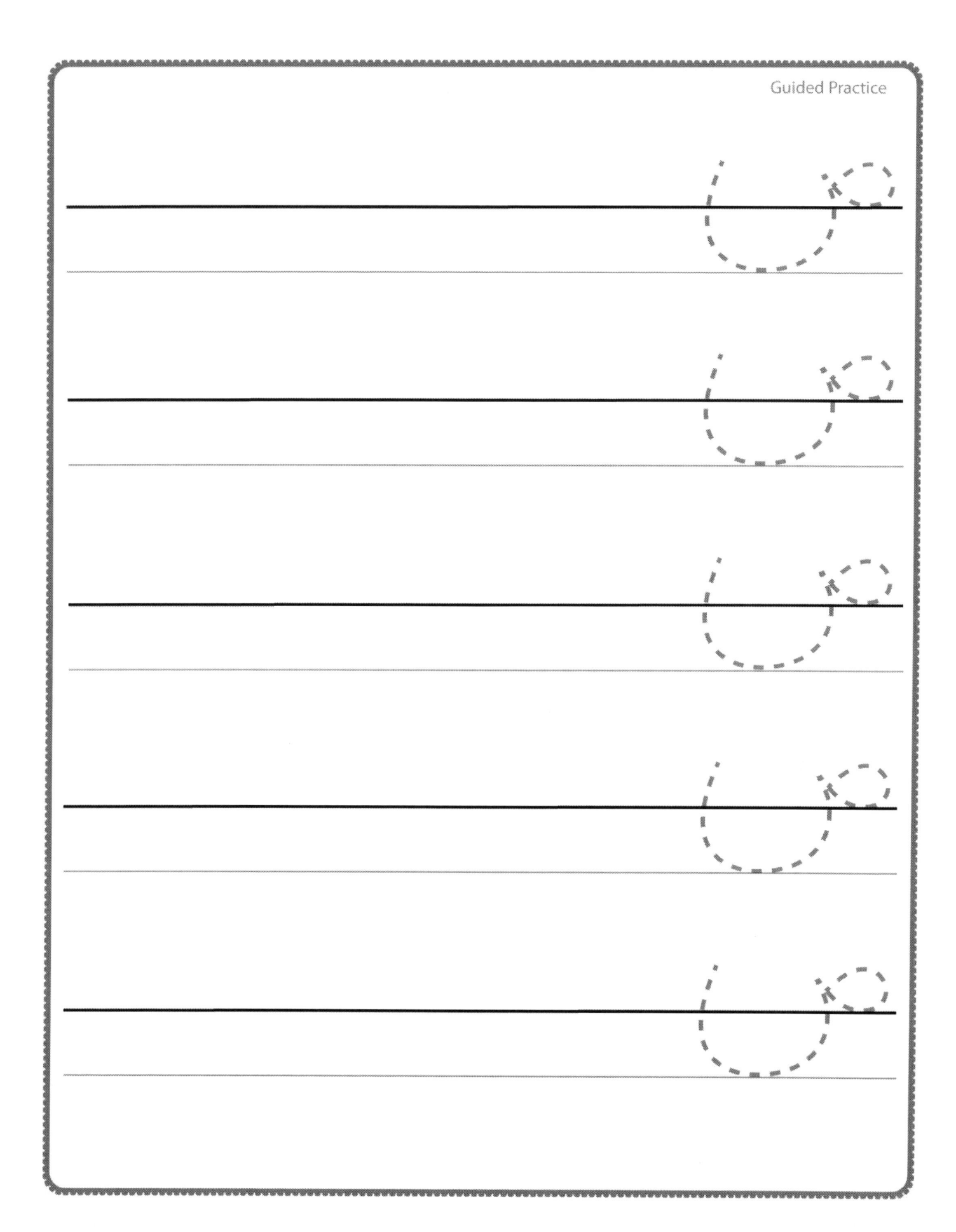

Guided Practice

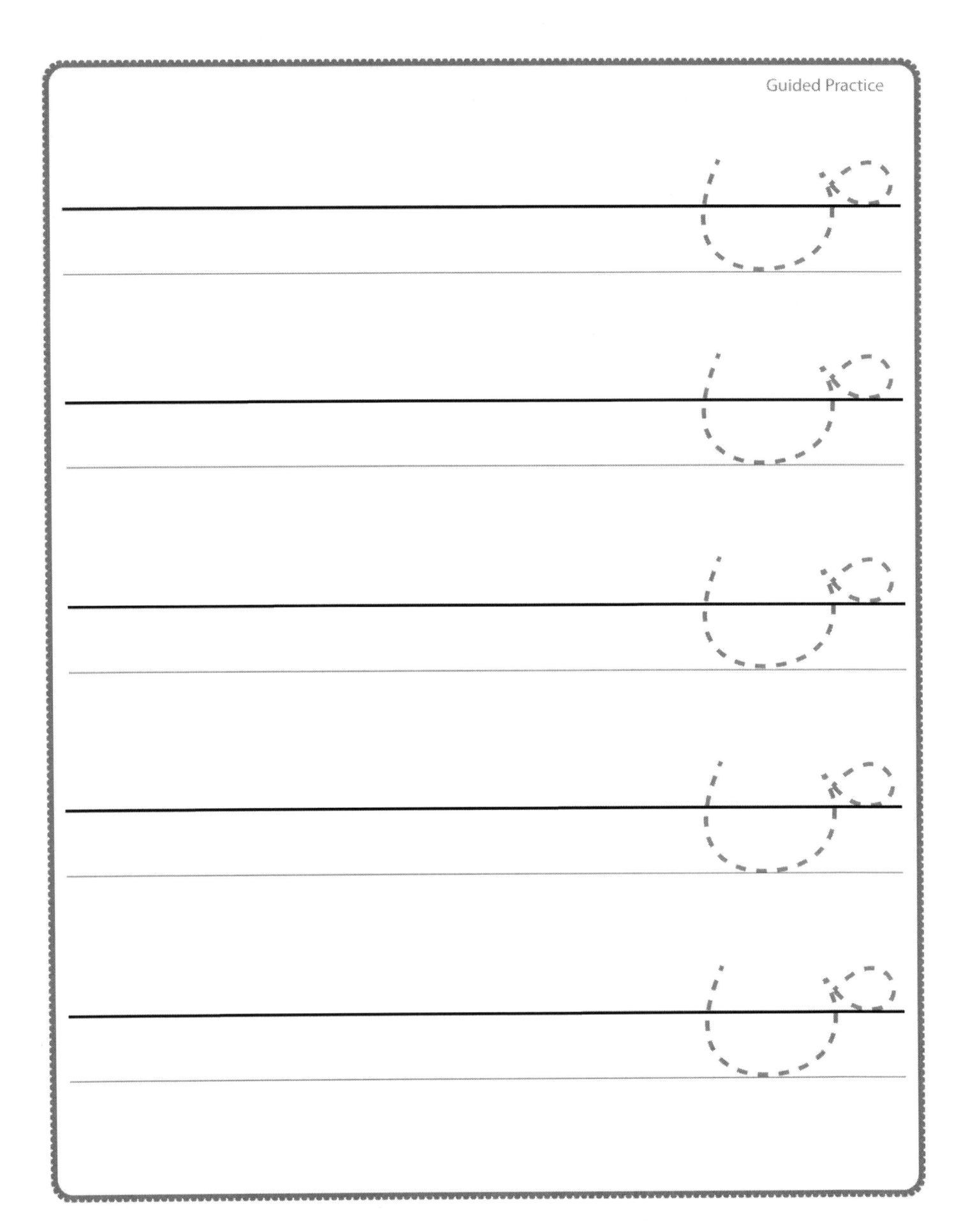

Guided Practice

Lesson: 15

How to write it:
The head of this letter rests on the line. Begin by drawing a loop, and then follow the arrow as it swoops under the line in a wide curve. Place a dot above the letter.

Dawd (dw)

ض

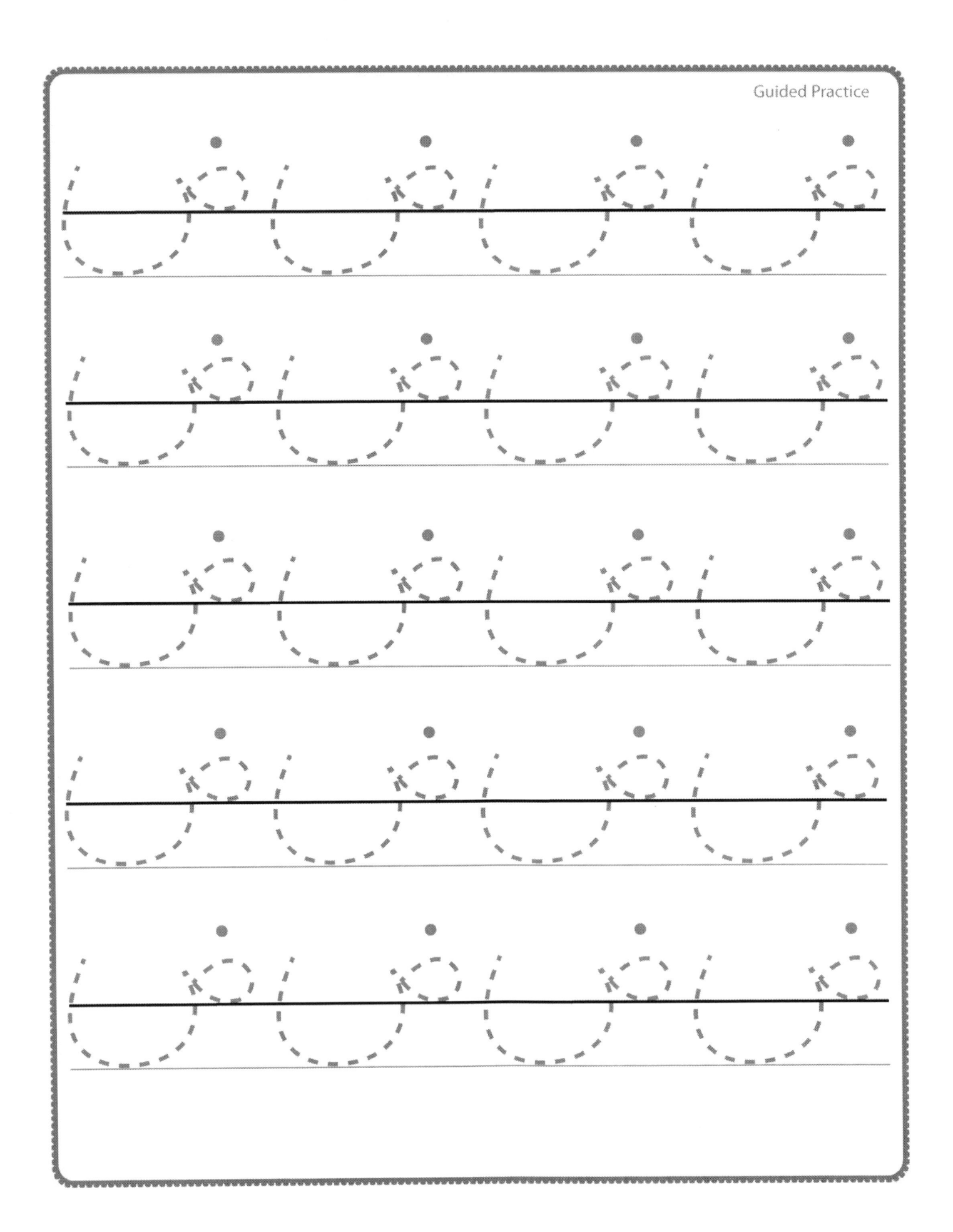

Guided Practice

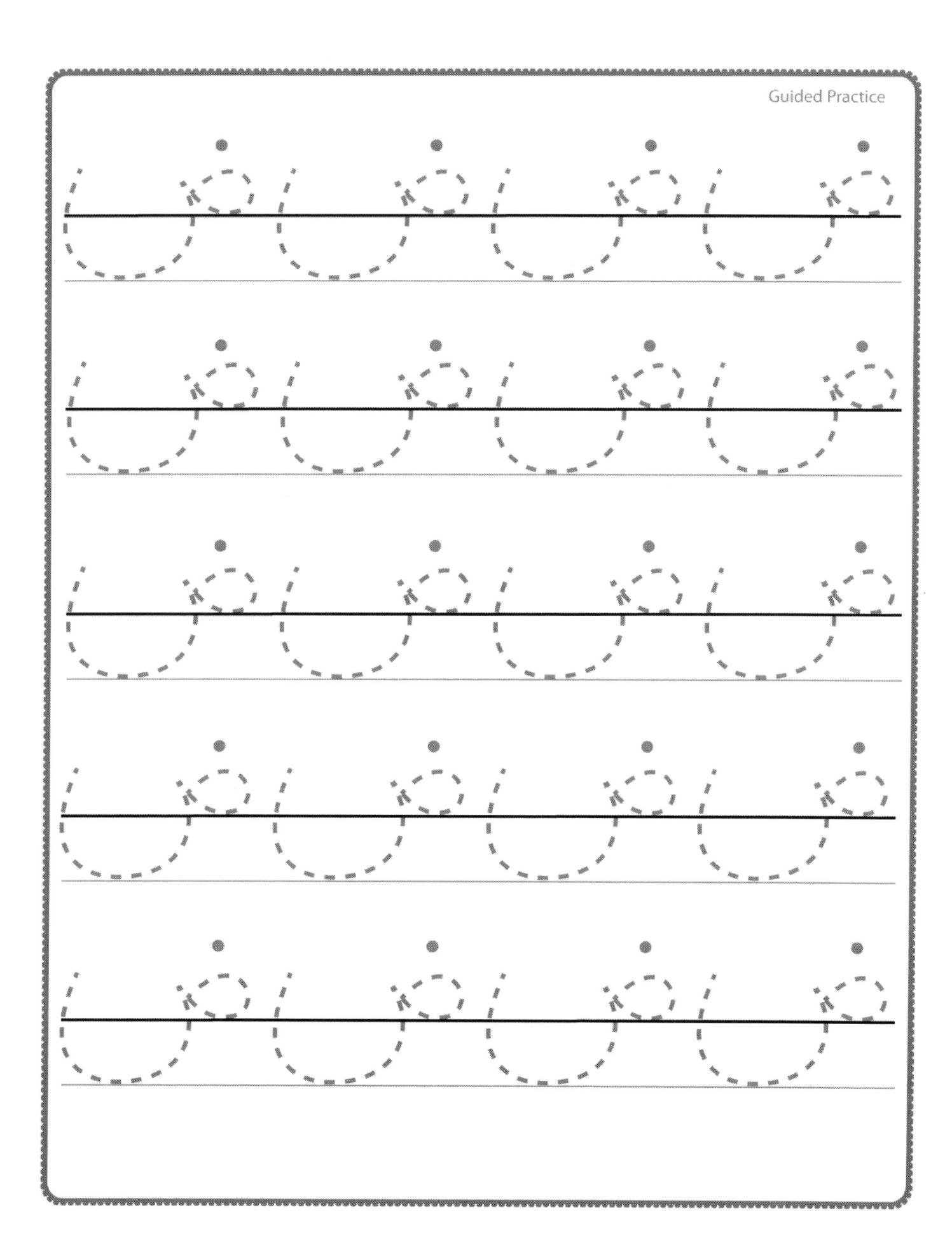

Guided Practice

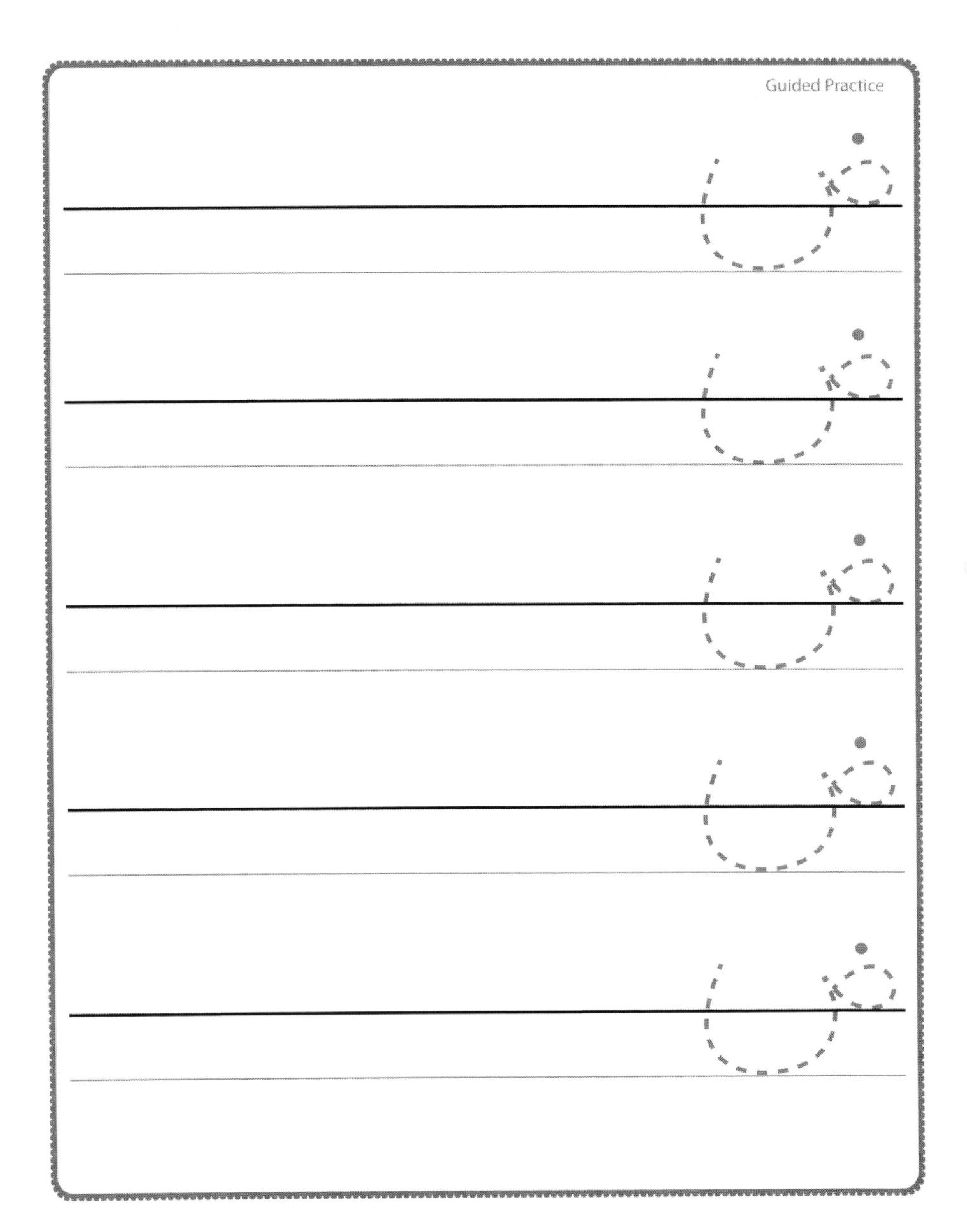

Guided Practice

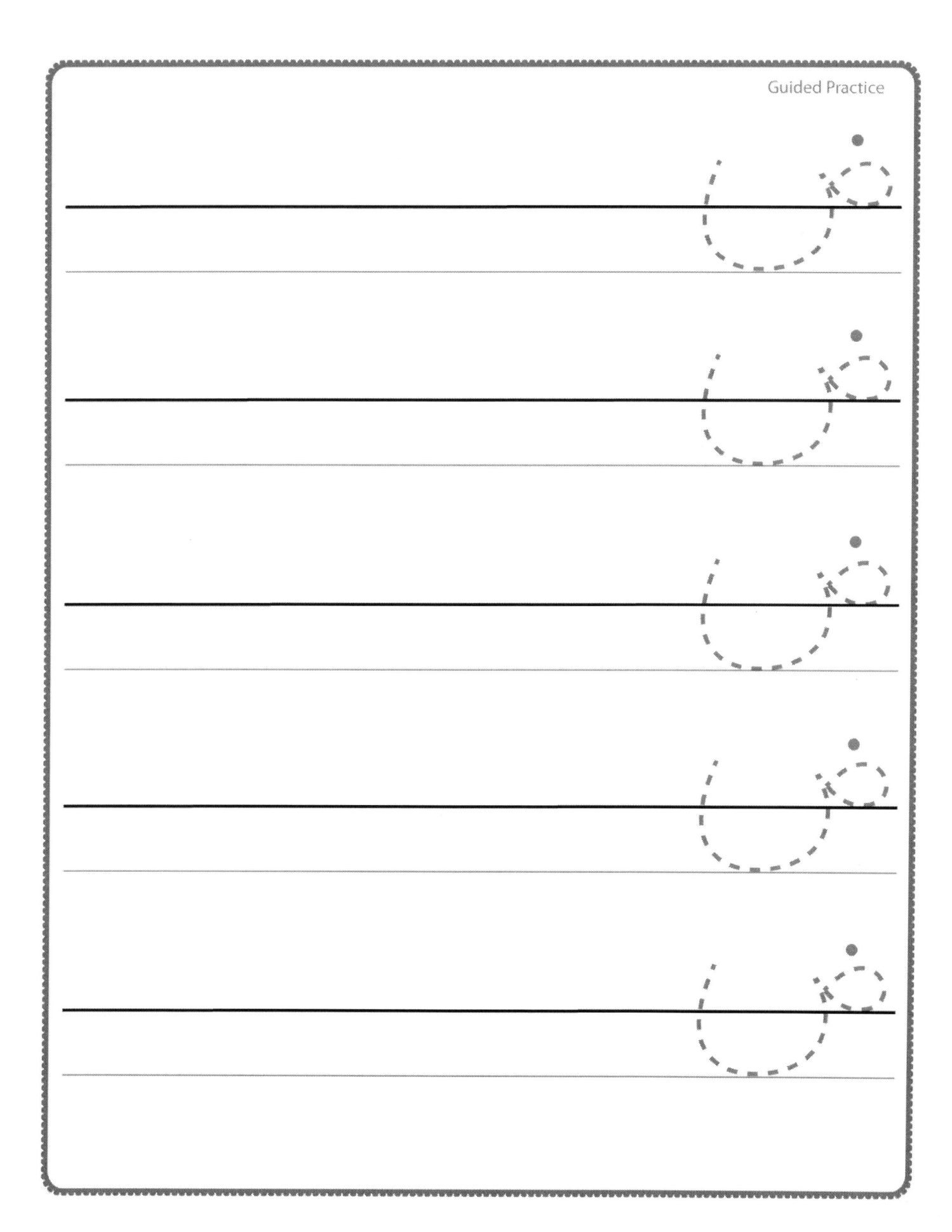

Guided Practice

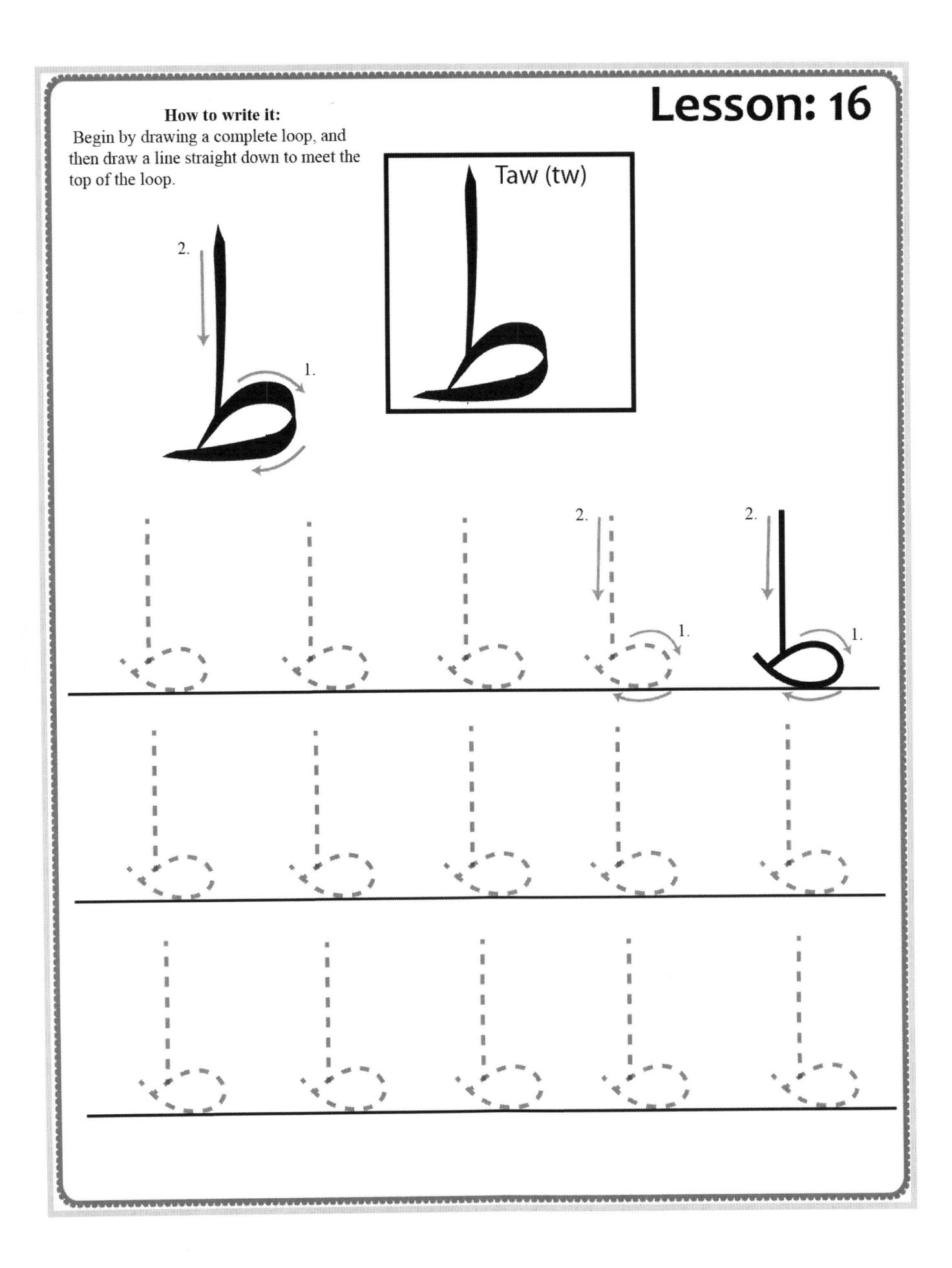

How to write it:
Begin by drawing a complete loop, and then draw a line straight down to meet the top of the loop.

Taw (tw)

Lesson: 16

Guided Practice

Guided Practice

Guided Practice

Guided Practice

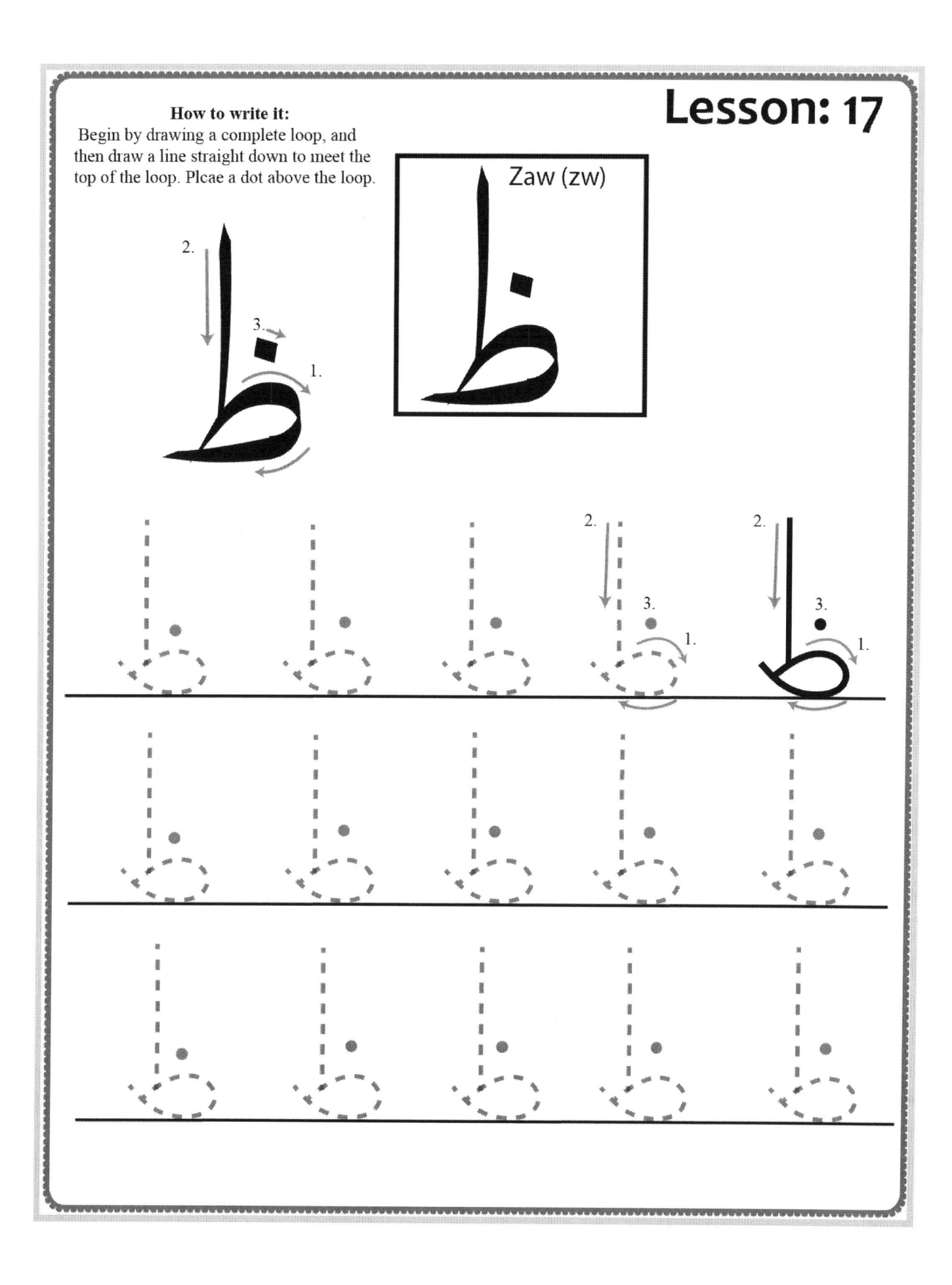

How to write it:
Begin by drawing a complete loop, and then draw a line straight down to meet the top of the loop. Plcae a dot above the loop.

Zaw (zw)

Lesson: 17

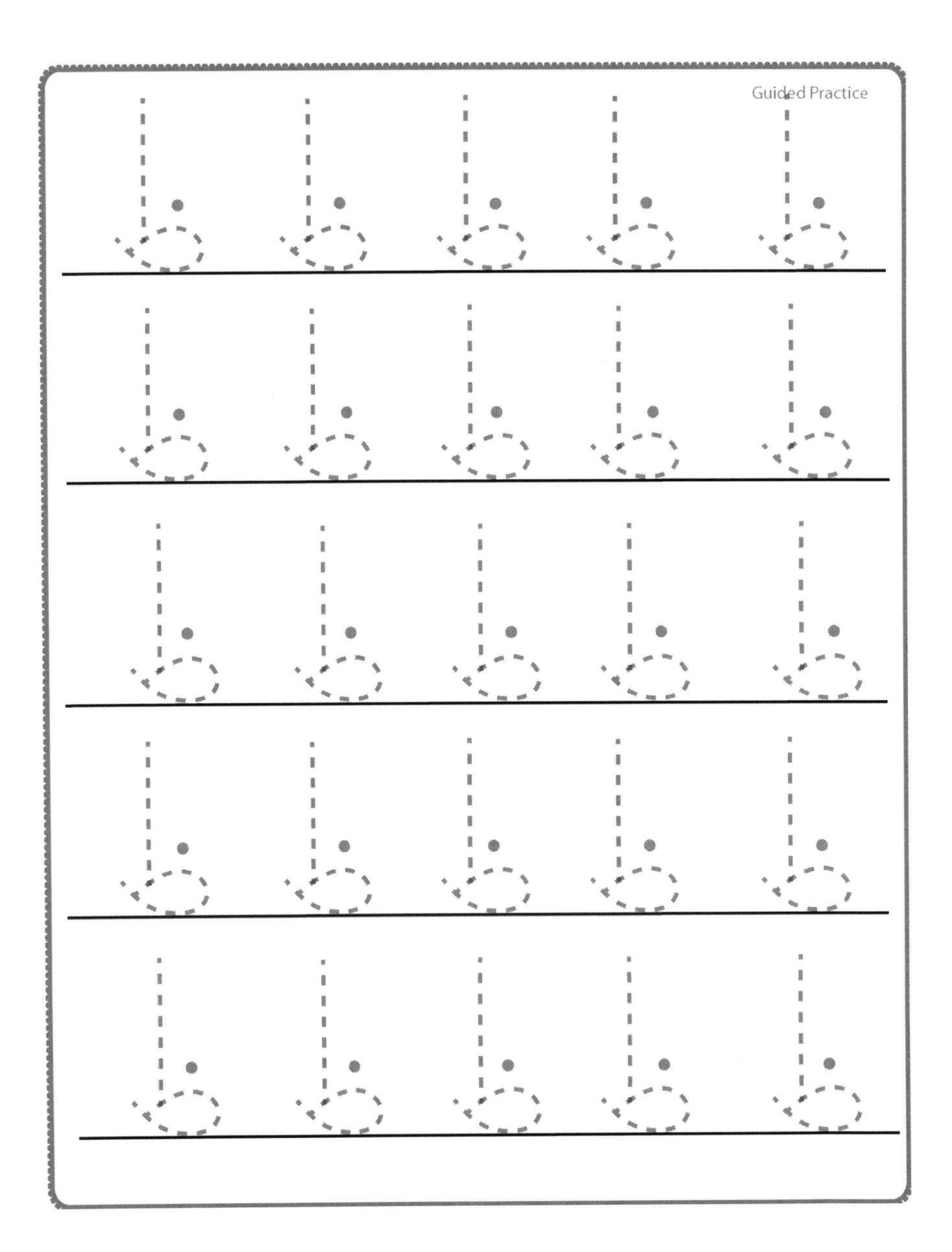

Guided Practice

Guided Practice

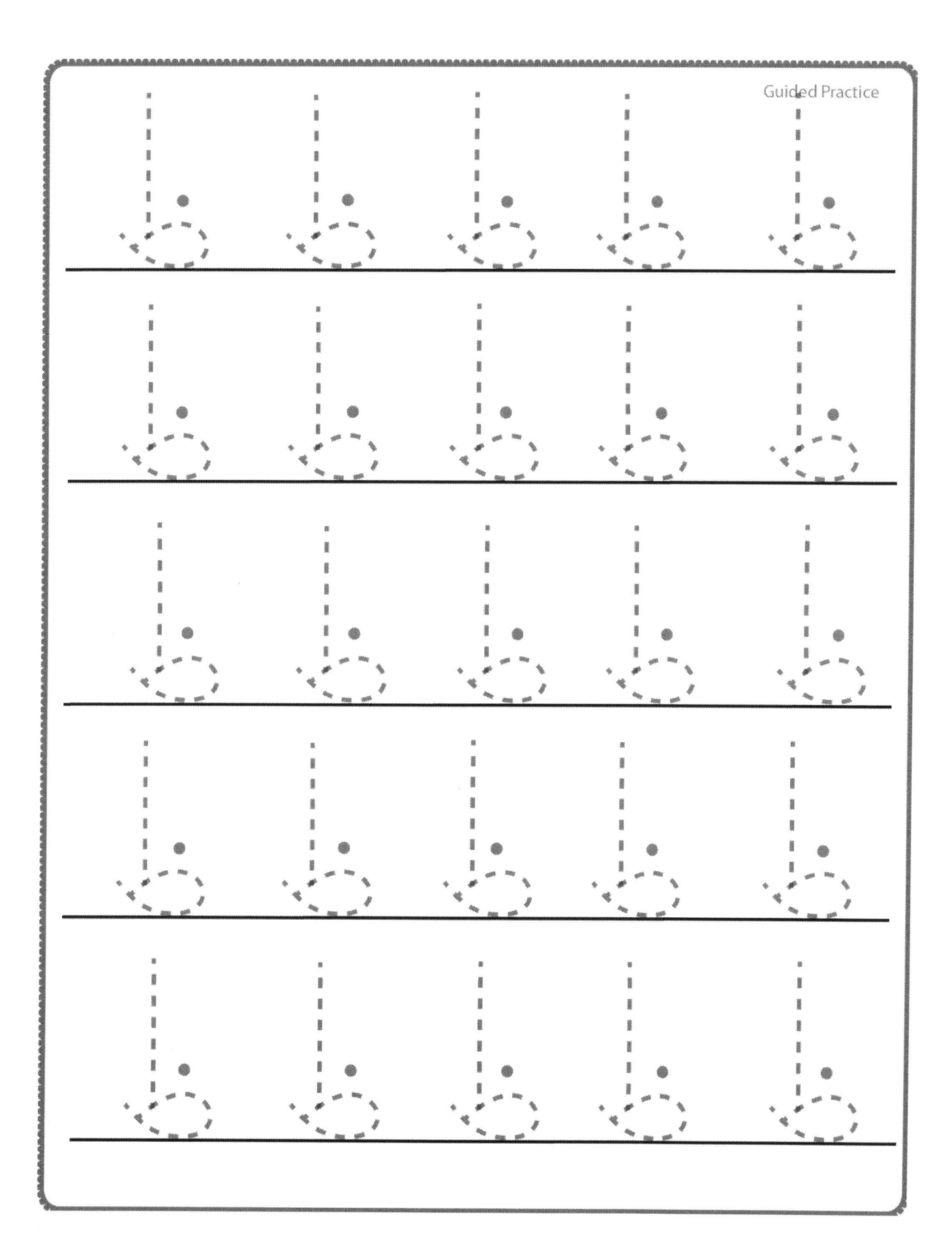

Guided Practice

Guided Practice

How to write it:
The head of this letter rests on the line. Begin with a curve for the head and follow the arrow around in a larger curve just under it.

Ayn ('a)

Lesson: 18

Guided Practice

c c c c c

d d d d d

d d d d d

d d d d

Guided Practice

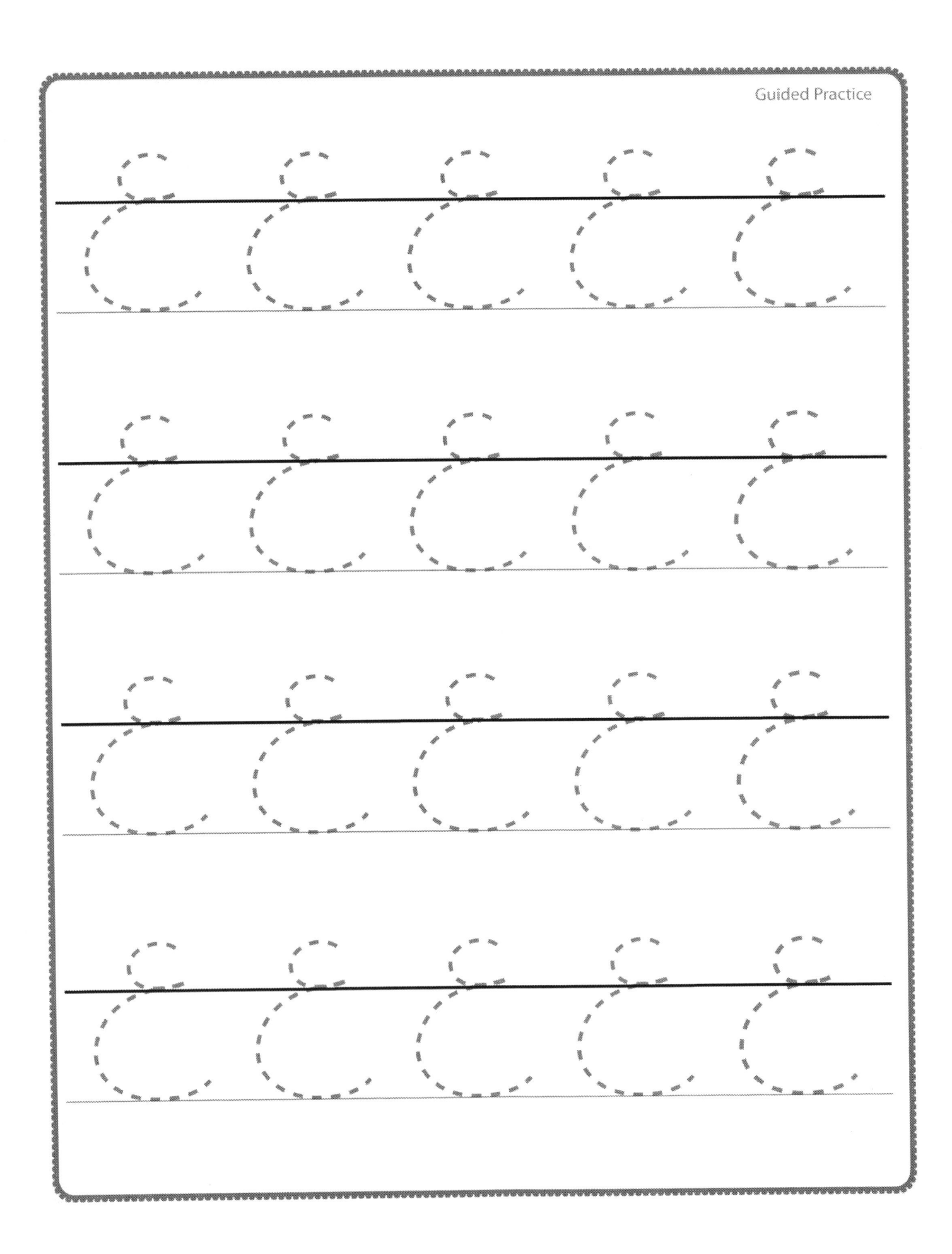

Guided Practice

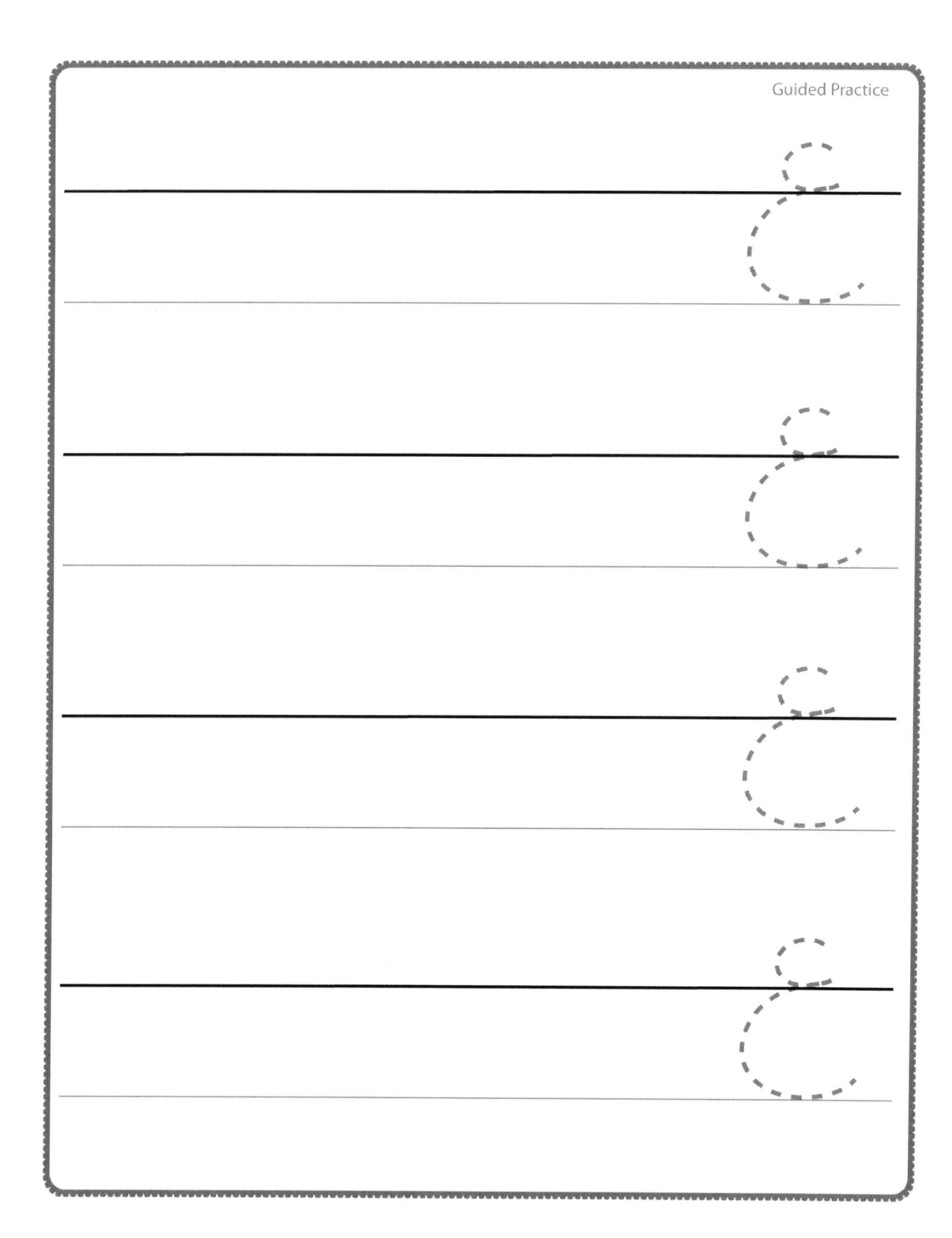

Guided Practice

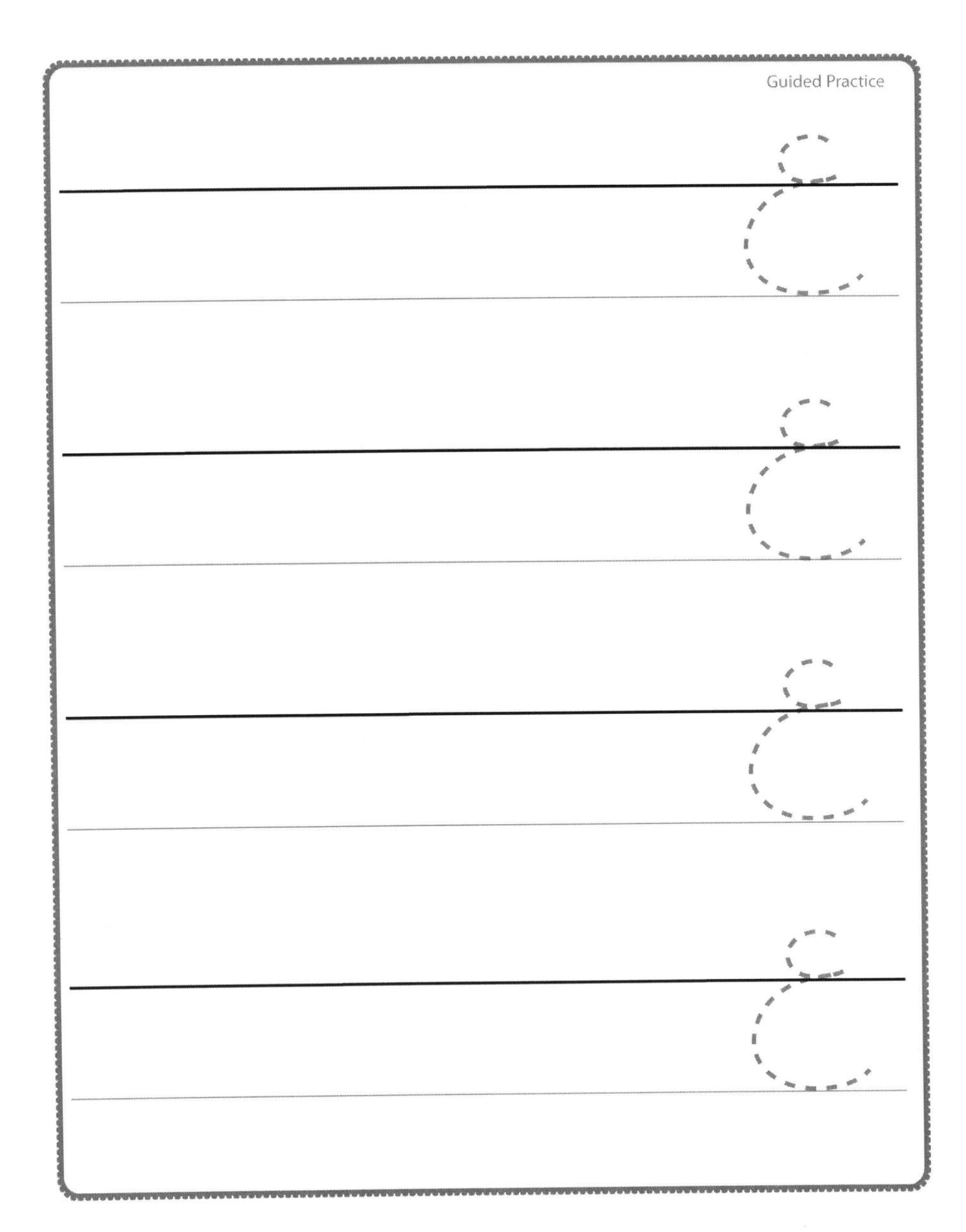

How to write it:
The head of this letter rests on the line. Begin with a curve for the head and follow the arrow around in a larger curve just under it. Draw a dot above the letter.

Gayn (g)

Lesson: 19

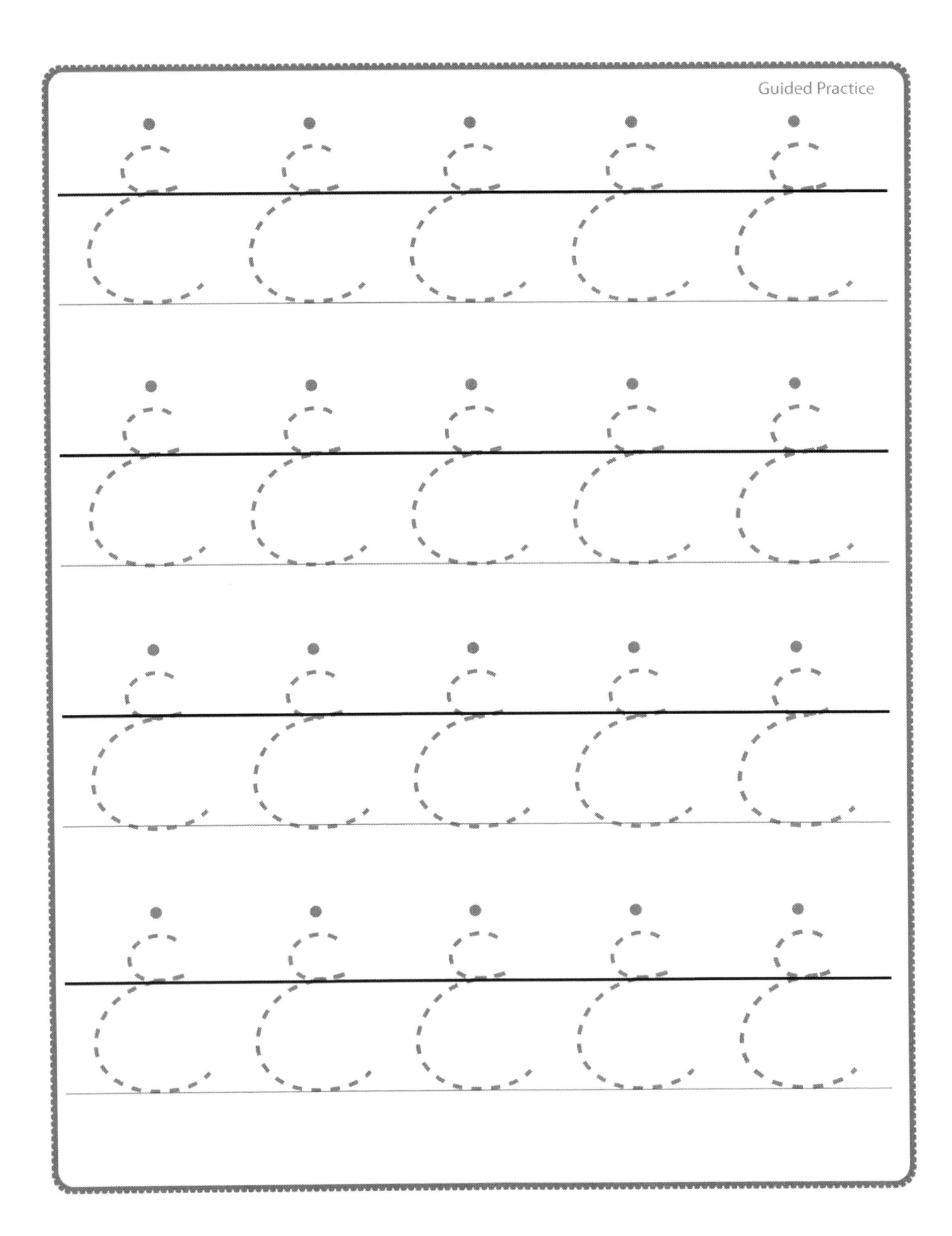

Guided Practice

Guided Practice

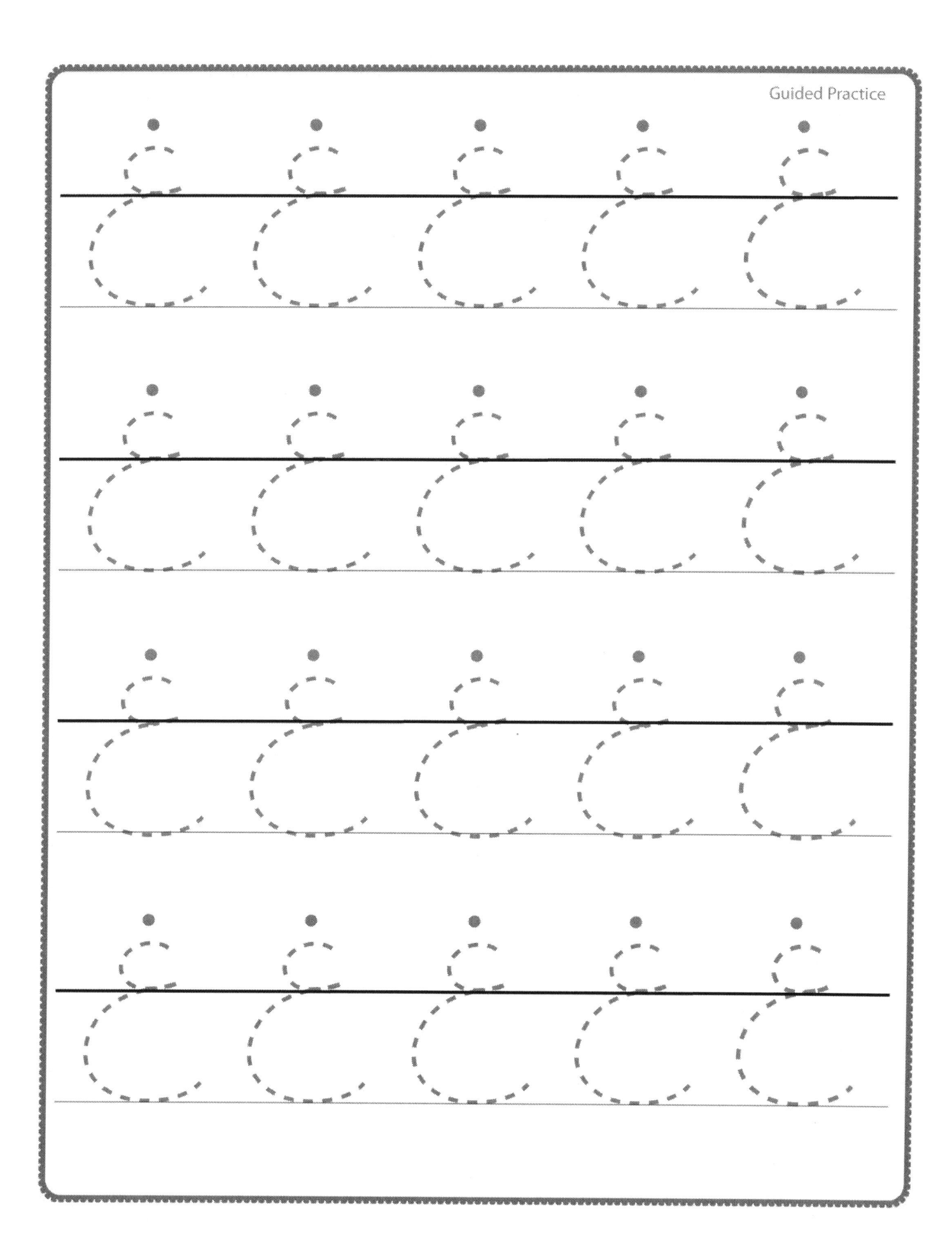

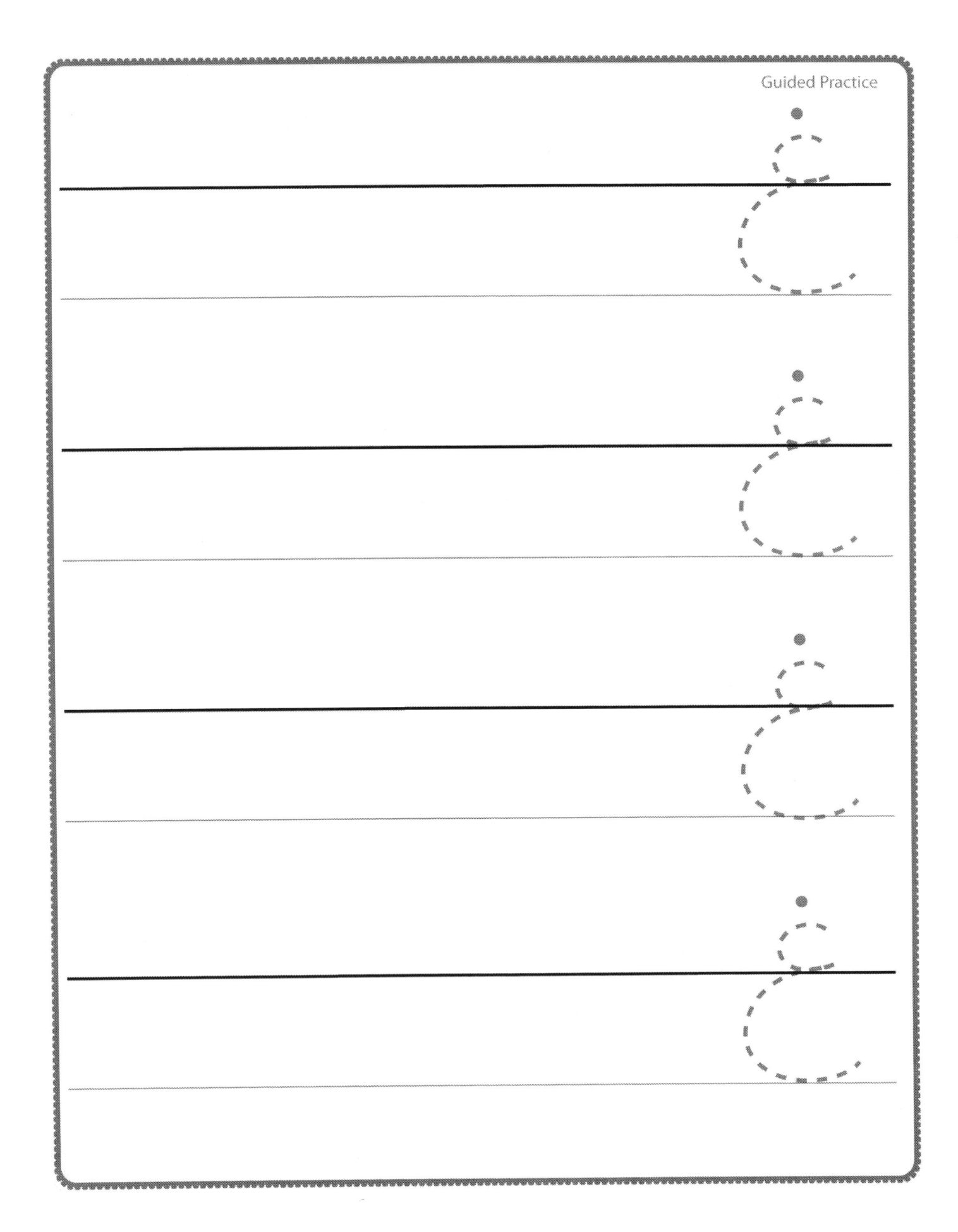

Guided Practice

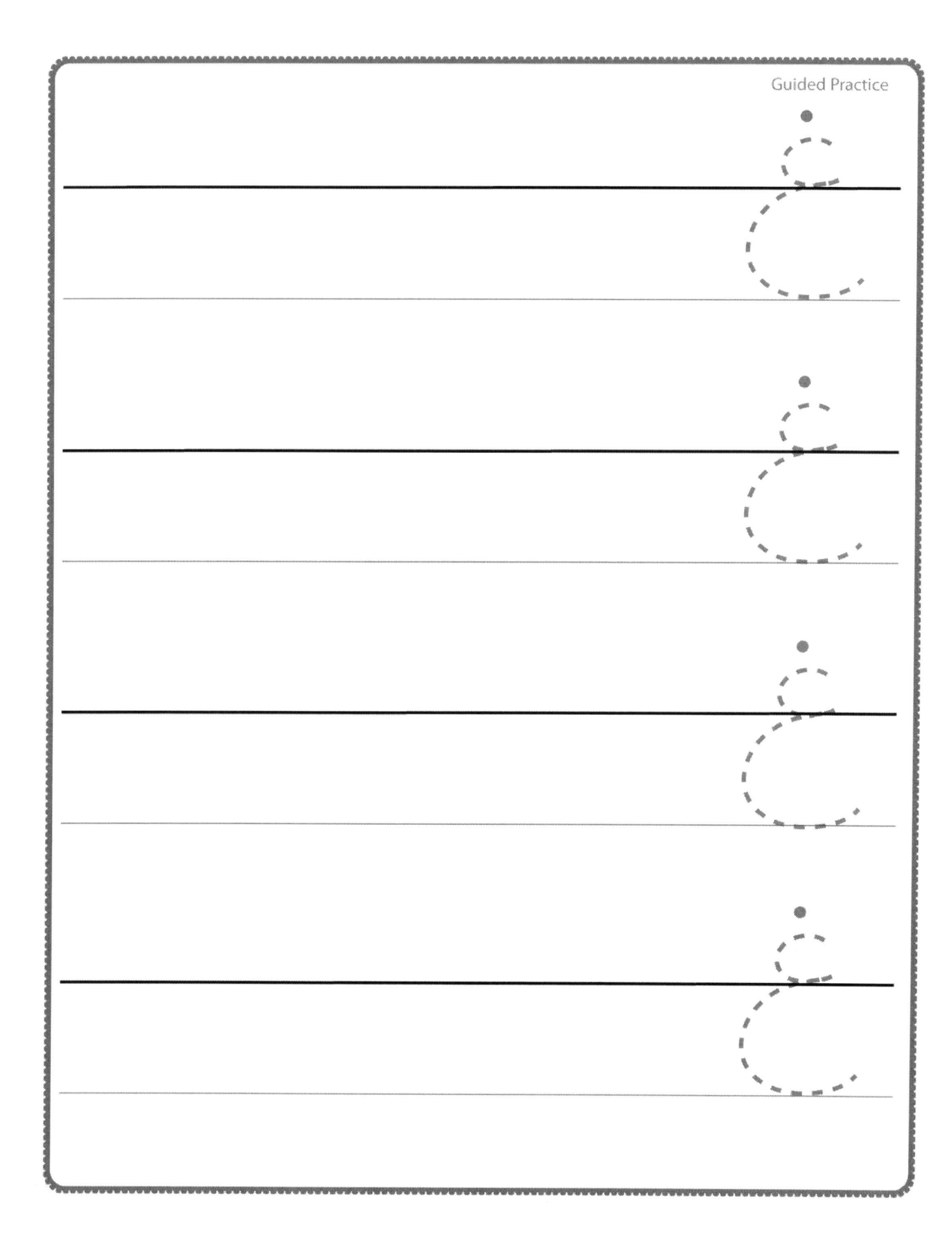

Guided Practice

Lesson: 20

How to write it:
Start by drawing a circle. Extend the tail end along the line towards the left and back up. Draw a dot above the letter.

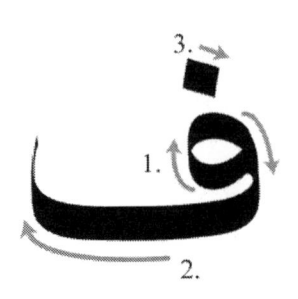

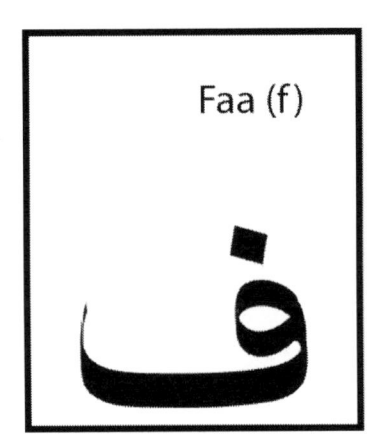

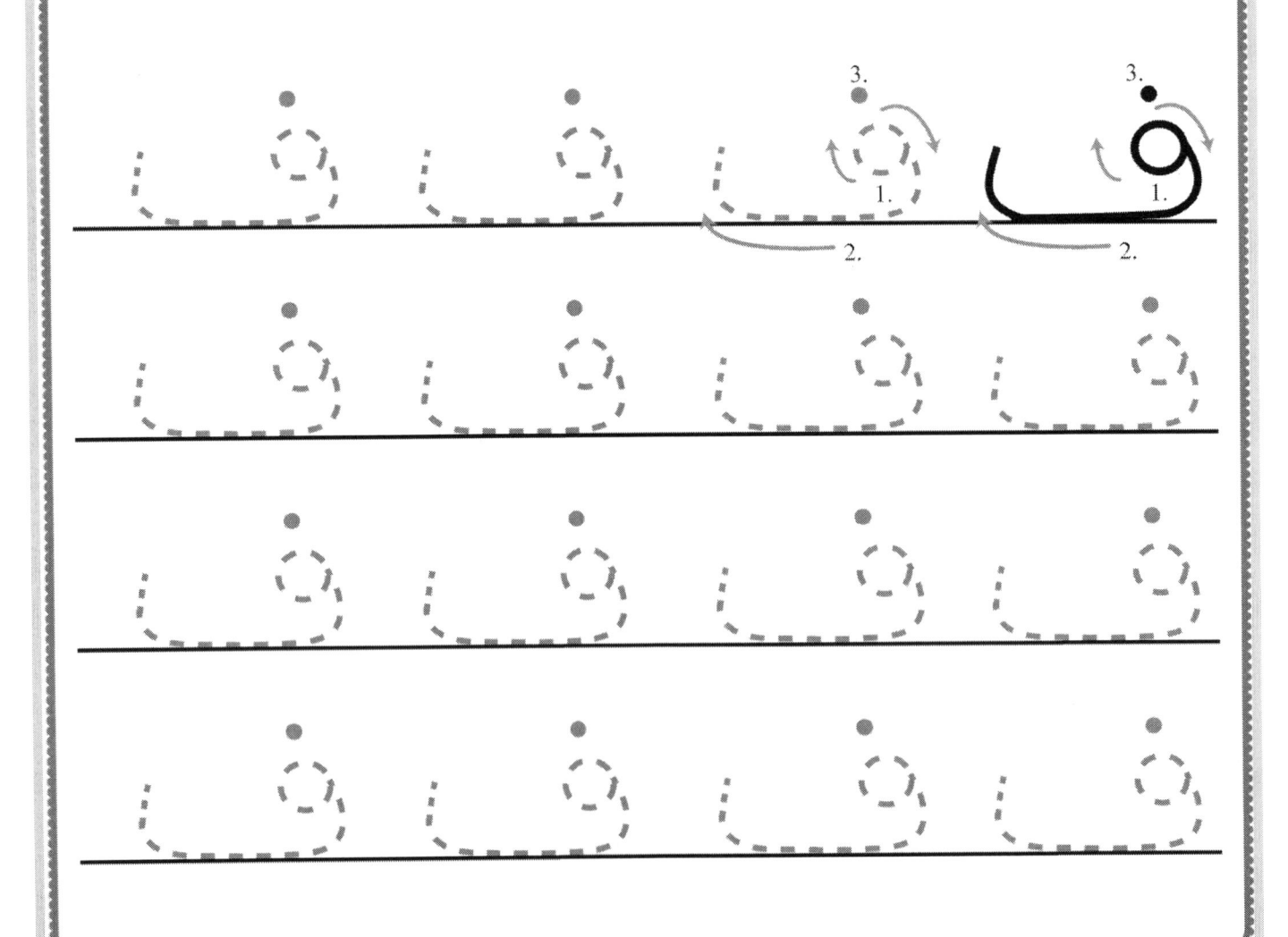

Faa (f)

ف

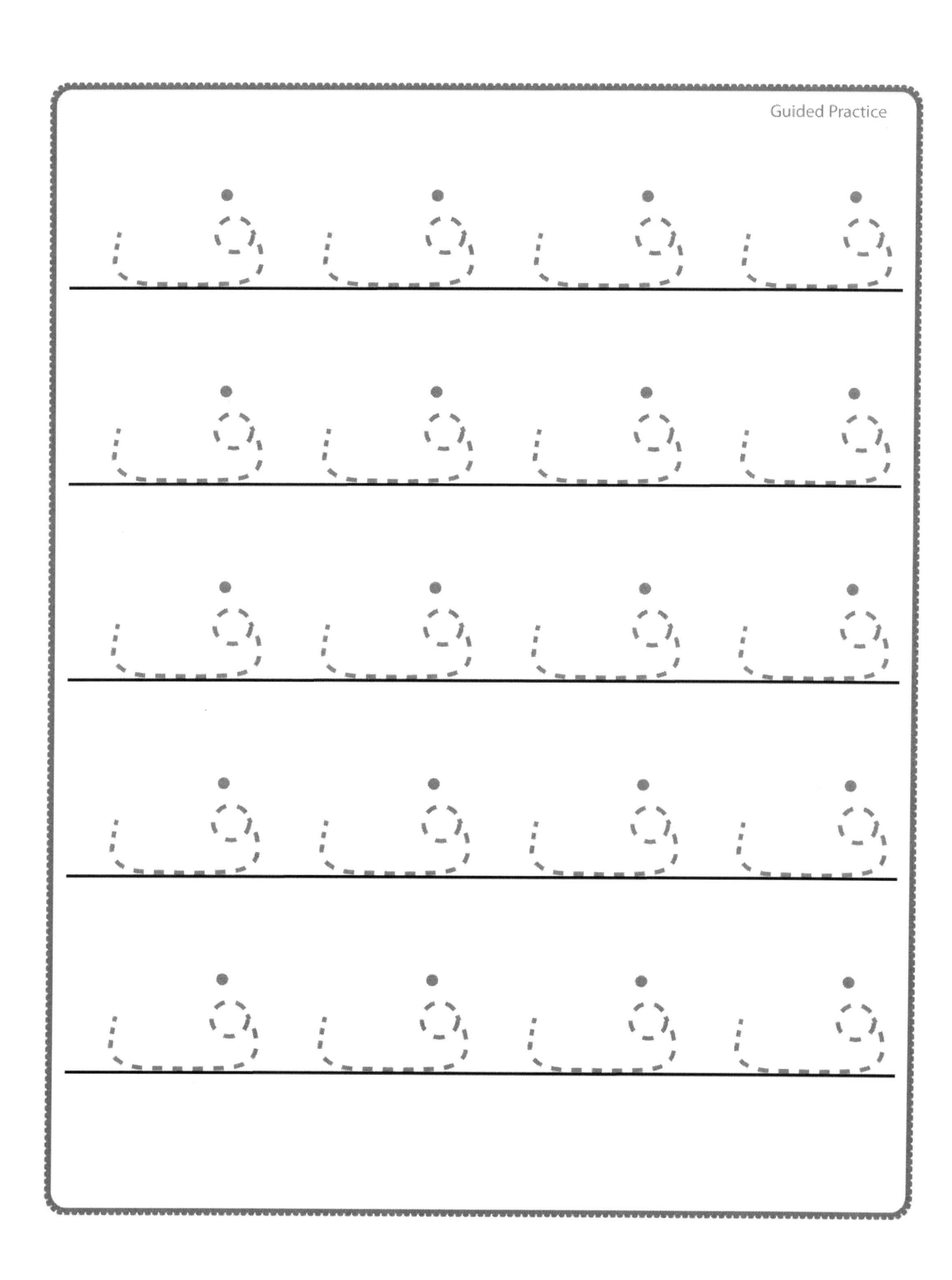

Guided Practice

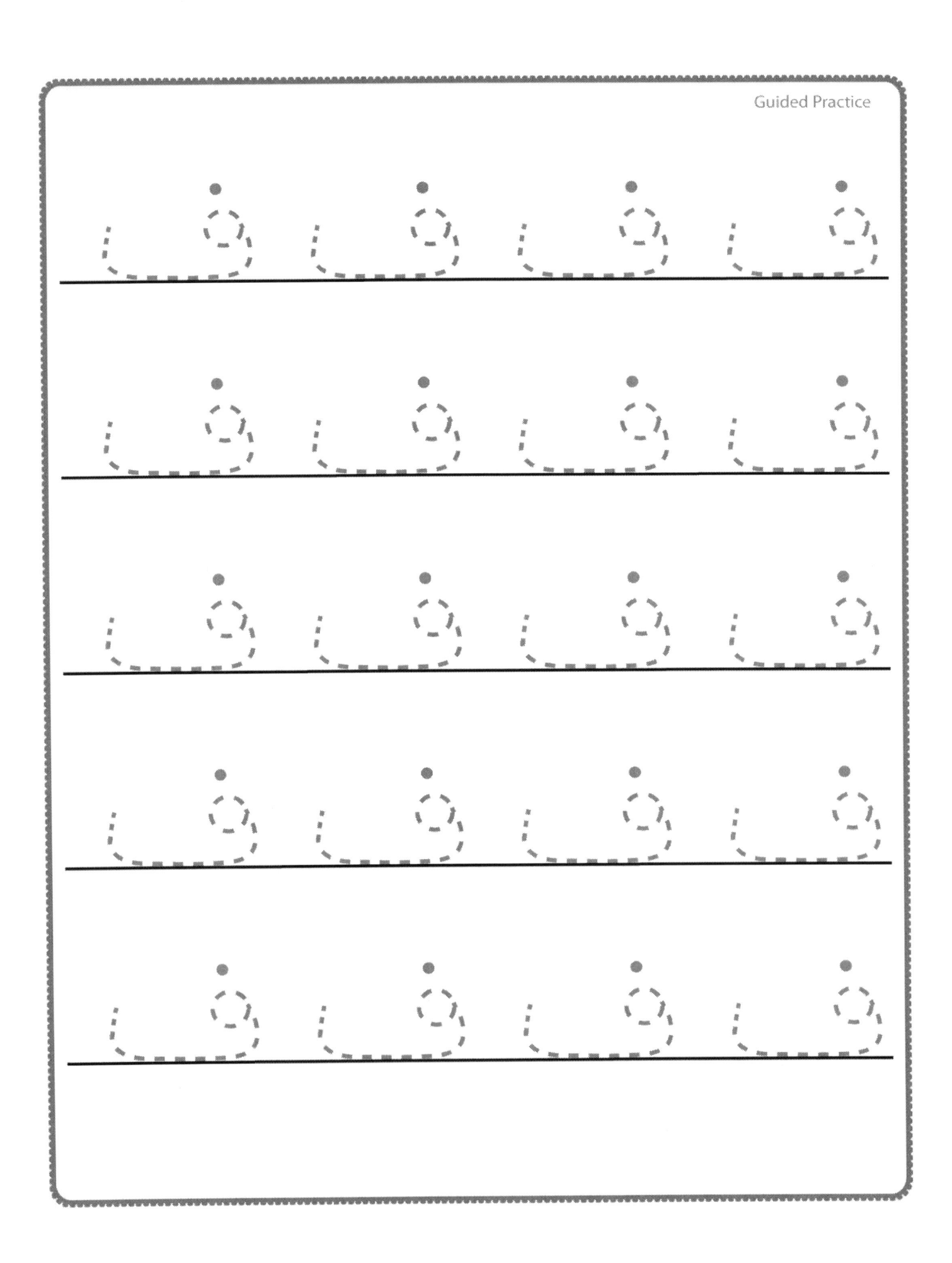

Guided Practice

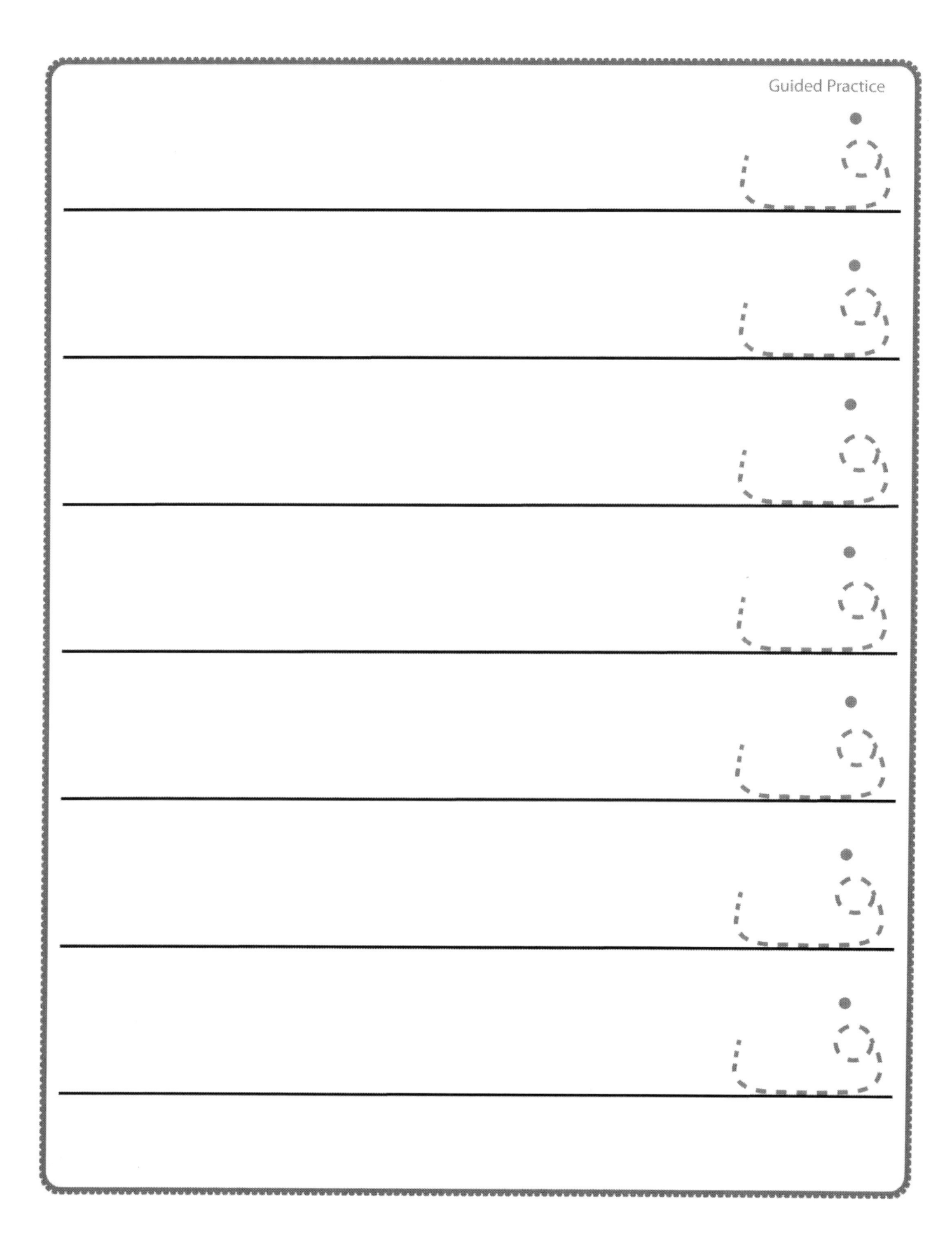

Guided Practice

Guided Practice

Lesson: 21

How to write it:
Start by drawing a circle. Extend the tail end in a wide circle under the line and back up. Draw two dots above the letter.

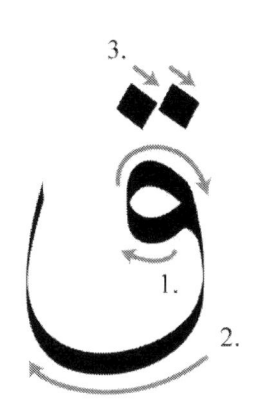

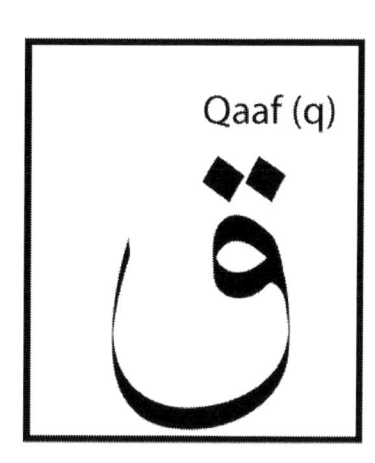

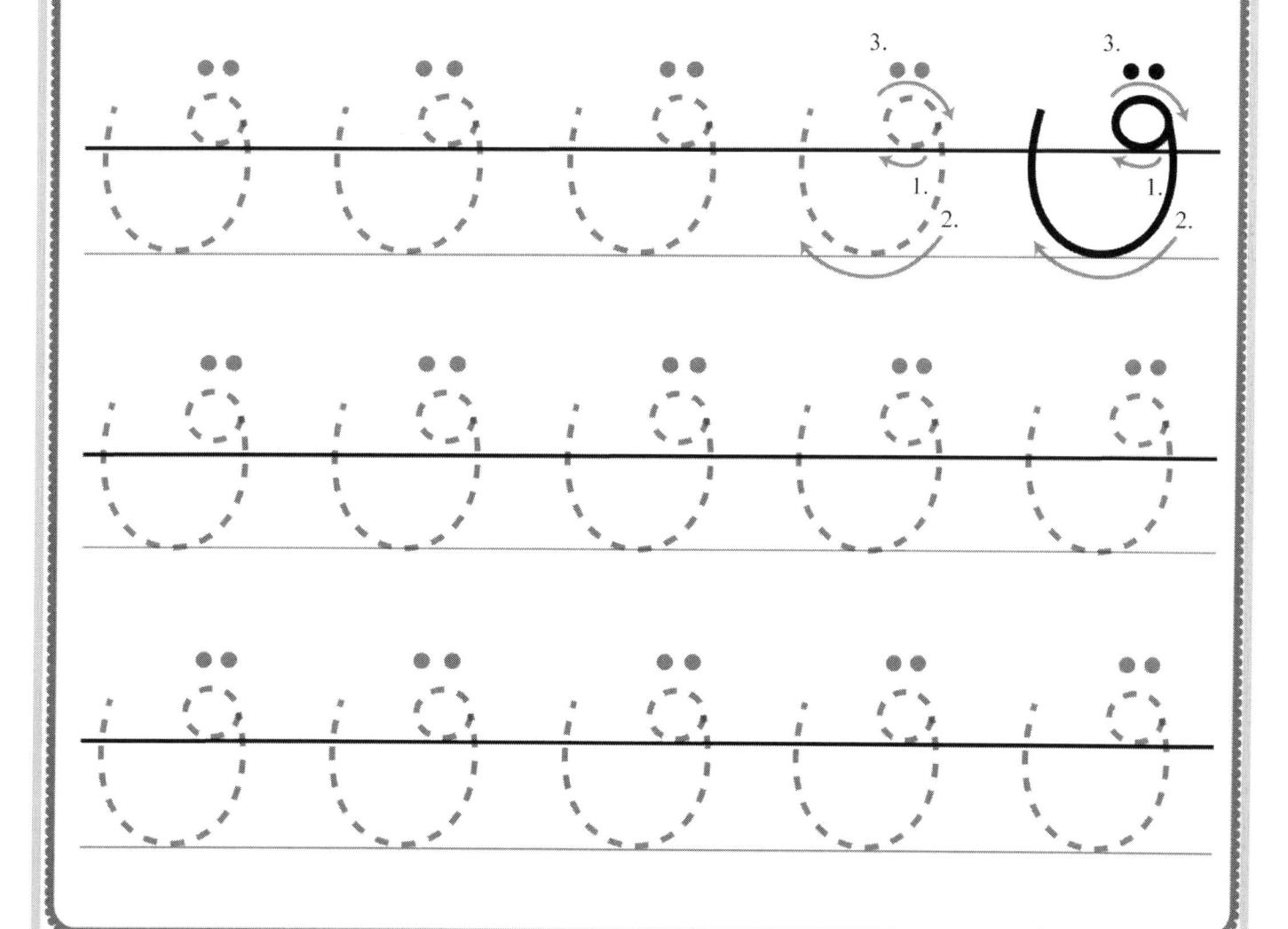

Qaaf (q)

ق

Guided Practice

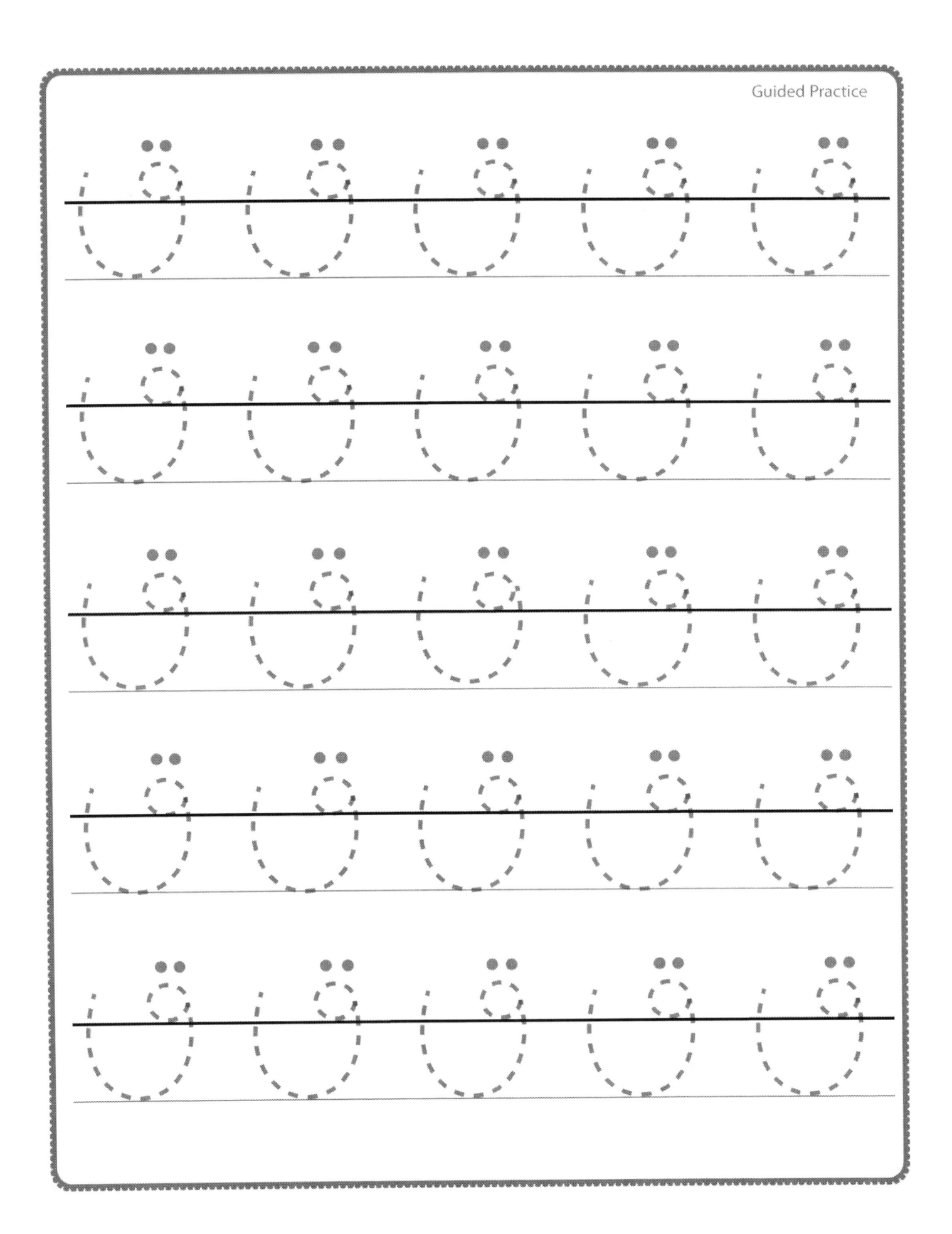

Guided Practice

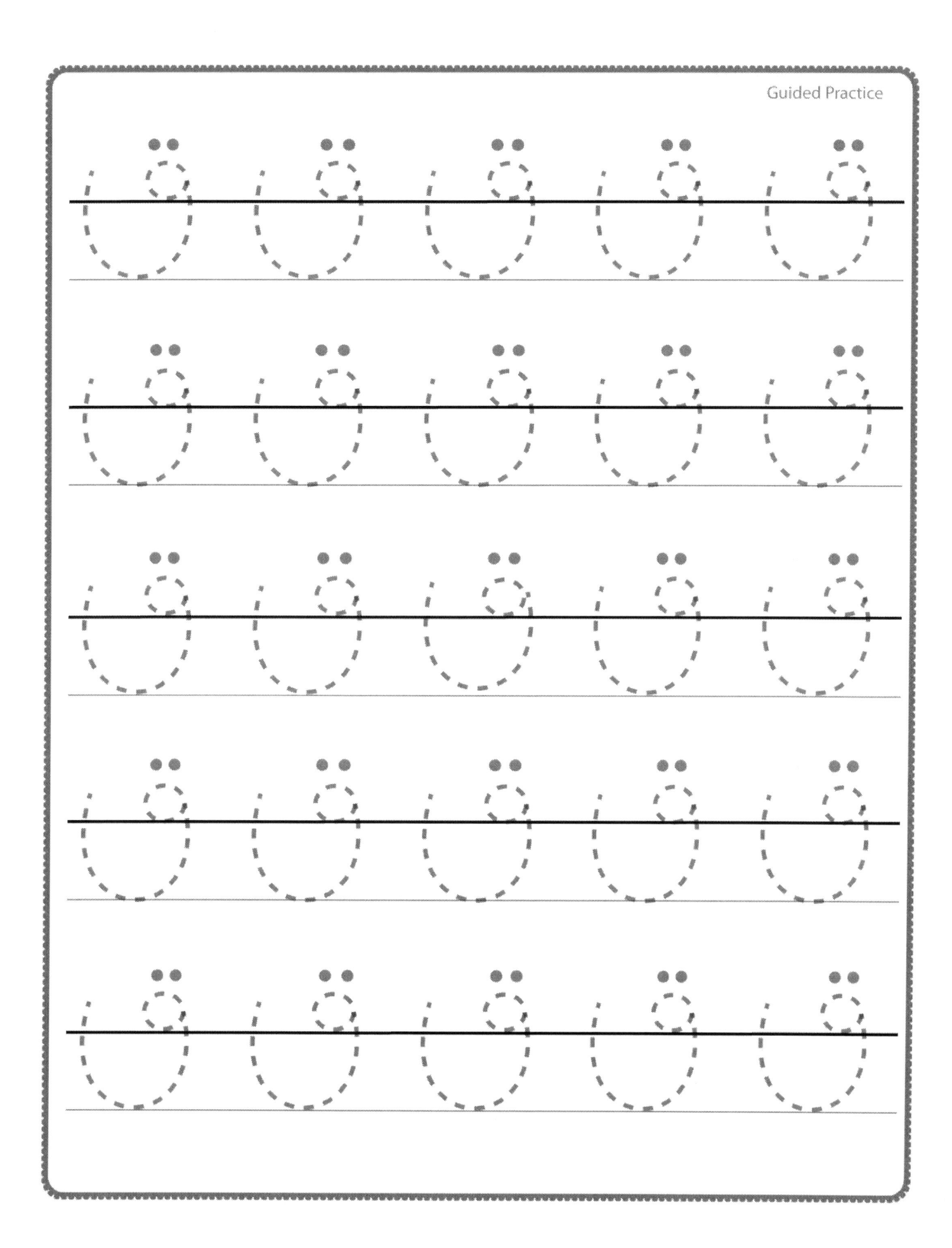

Guided Practice

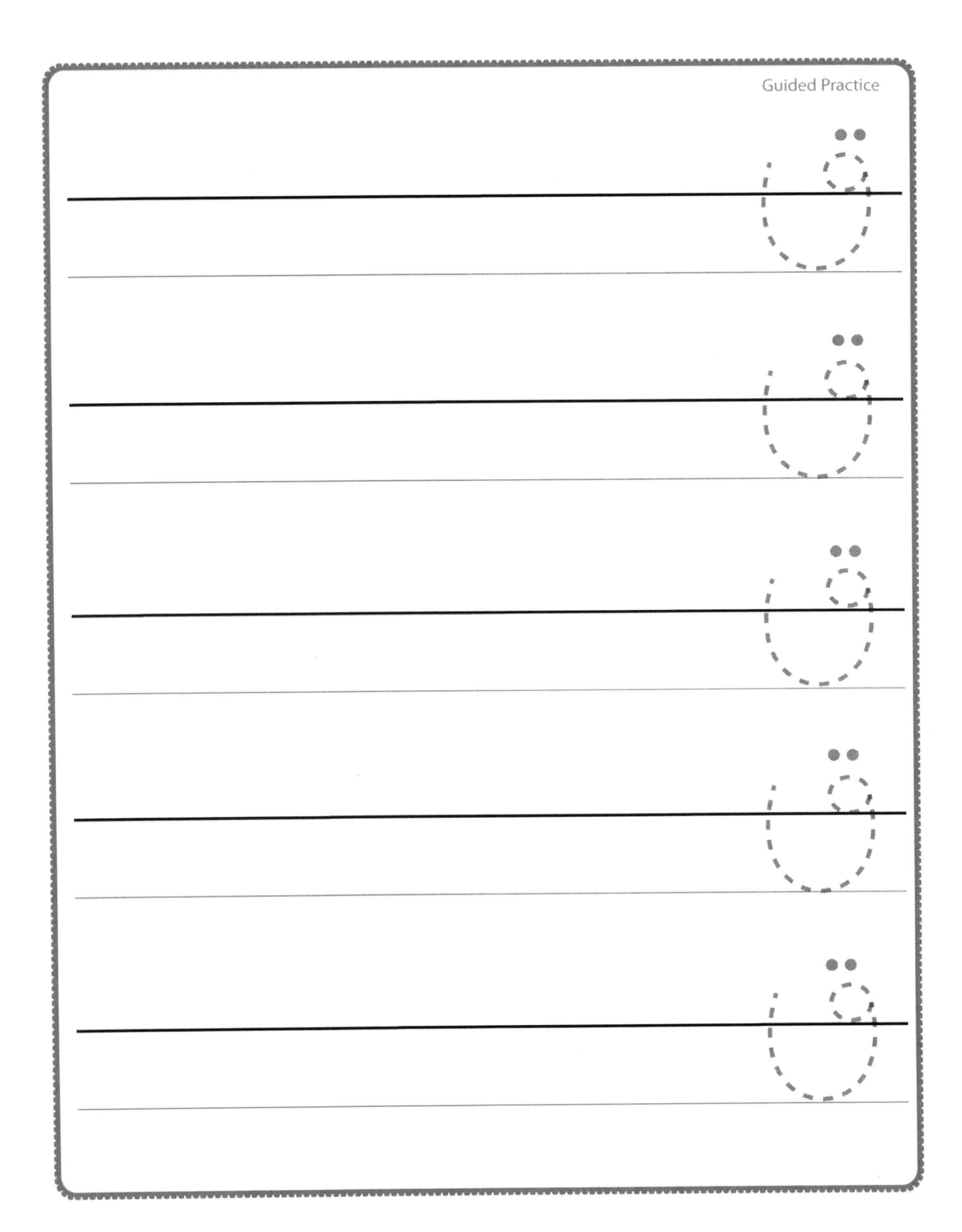

Guided Practice

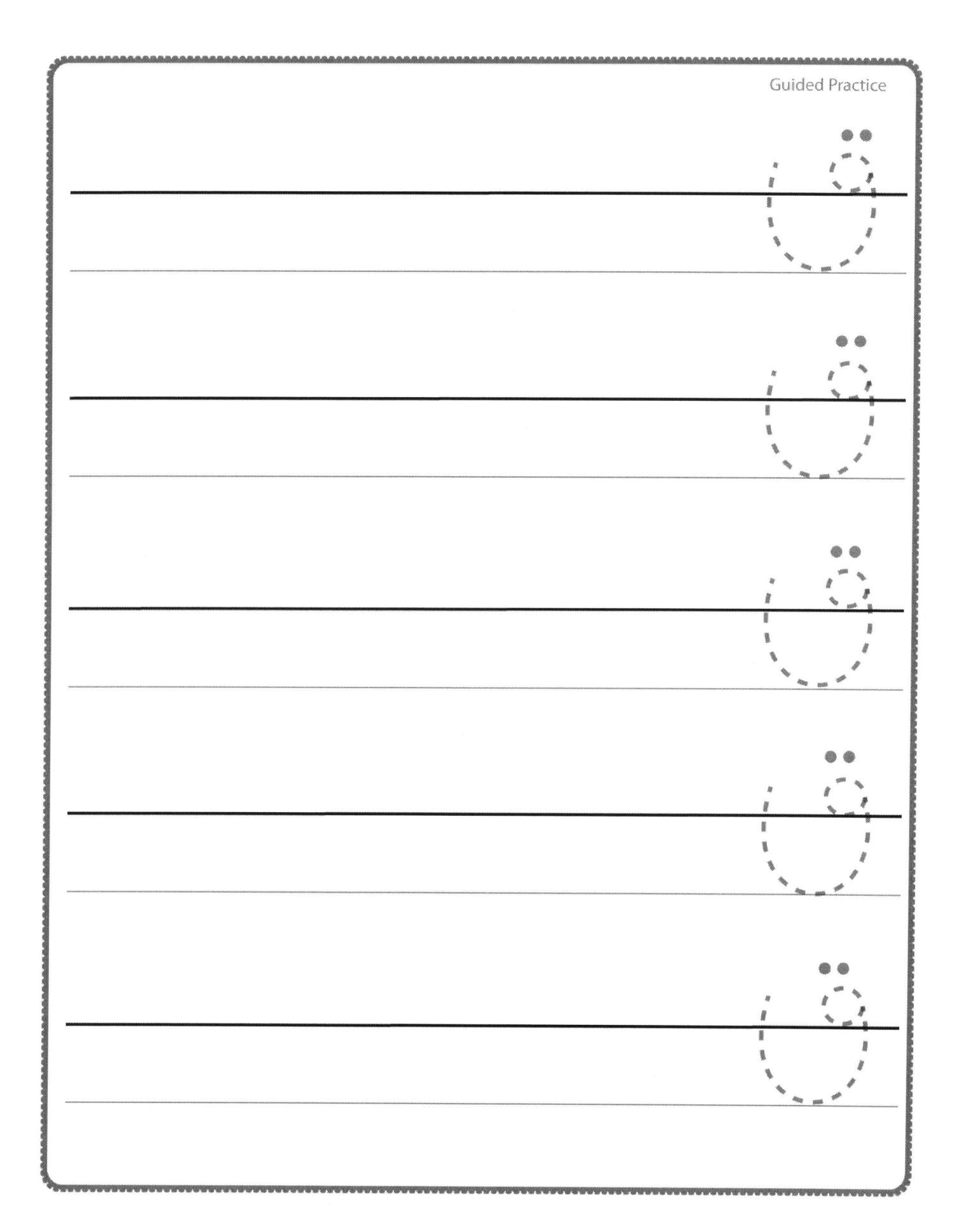

Lesson: 22

How to write it:
Begin by drawing a straight line down, and then follow the arrows across the bottom in a straight line. Finish by drawing an s-shaped swirl inside the letter.

Kaaf (k)

Guided Practice

Guided Practice

Guided Practice

Guided Practice

Lesson: 23

How to write it:
Start by drawing a line straight down.
Extend the tail around in a loop.

Laam (l)

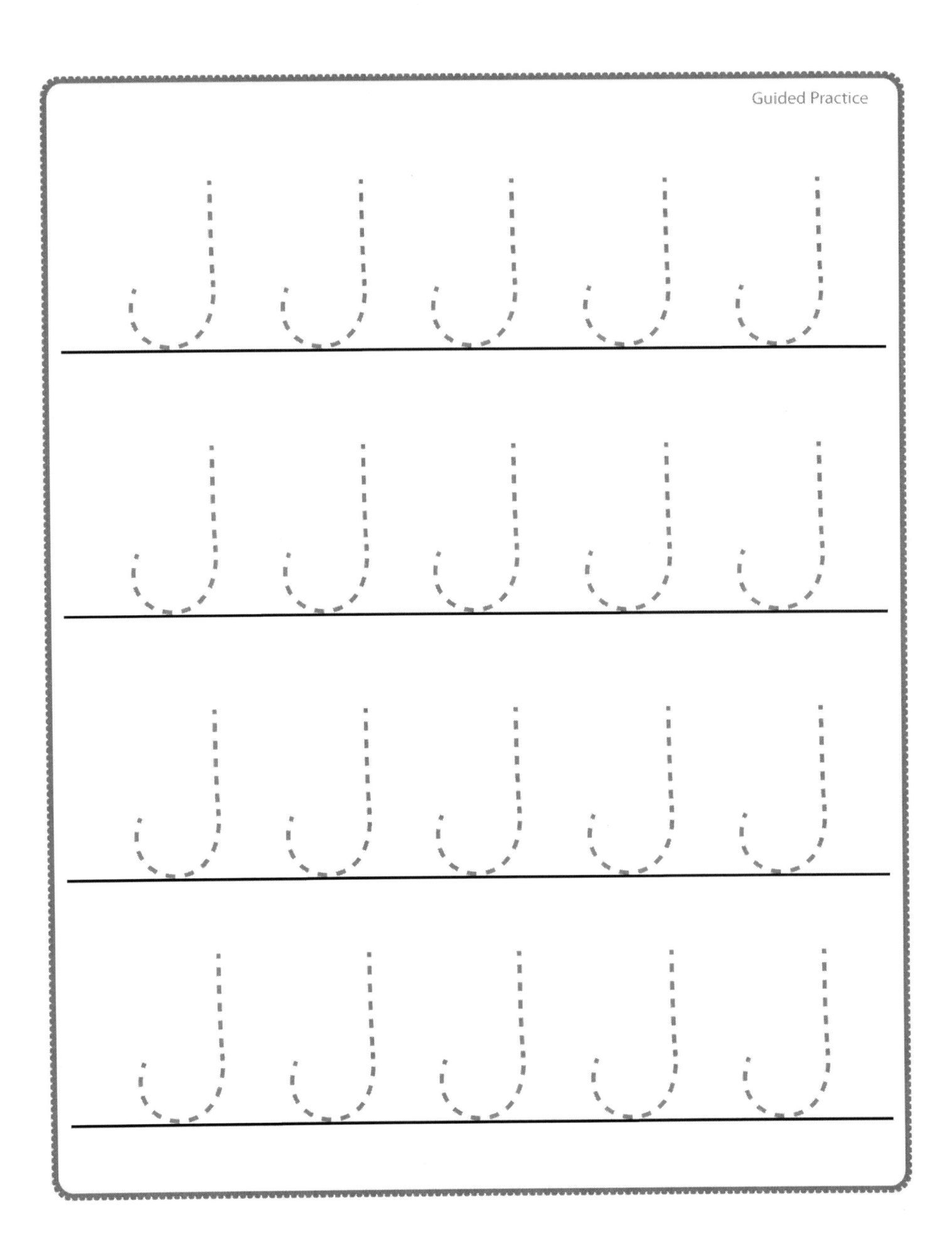

Guided Practice

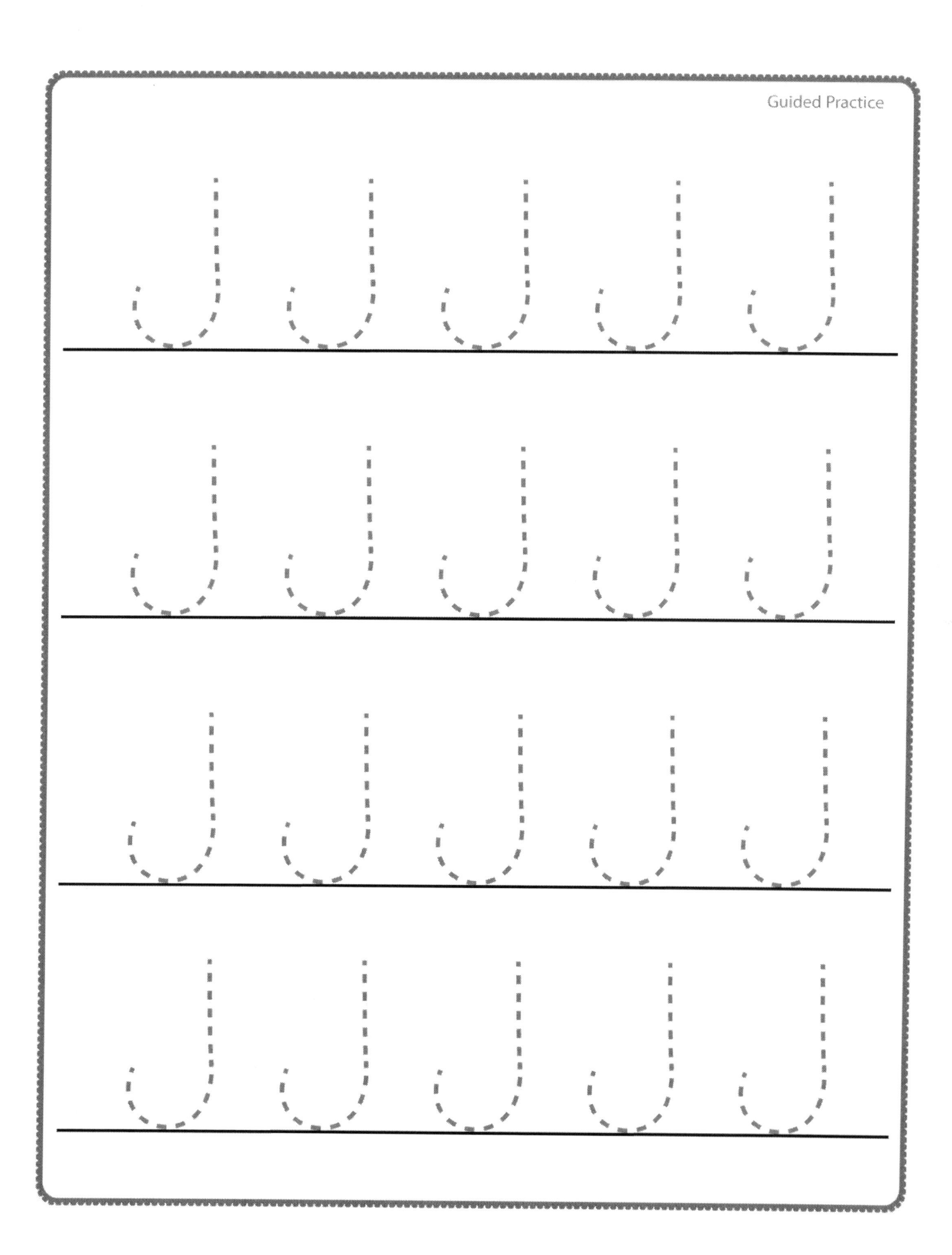

Guided Practice

Guided Practice

Guided Practice

Lesson: 24

How to write it:
Start by drawing a circle. Extend the tail end straight down below the line.

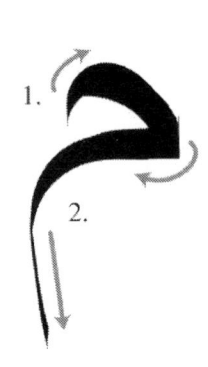

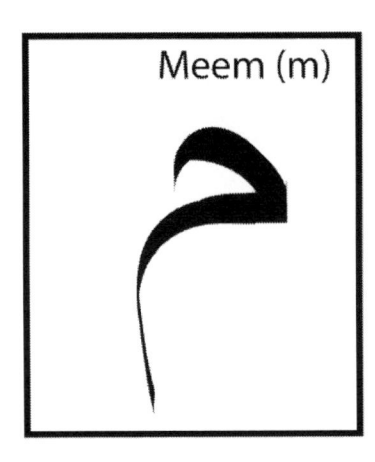

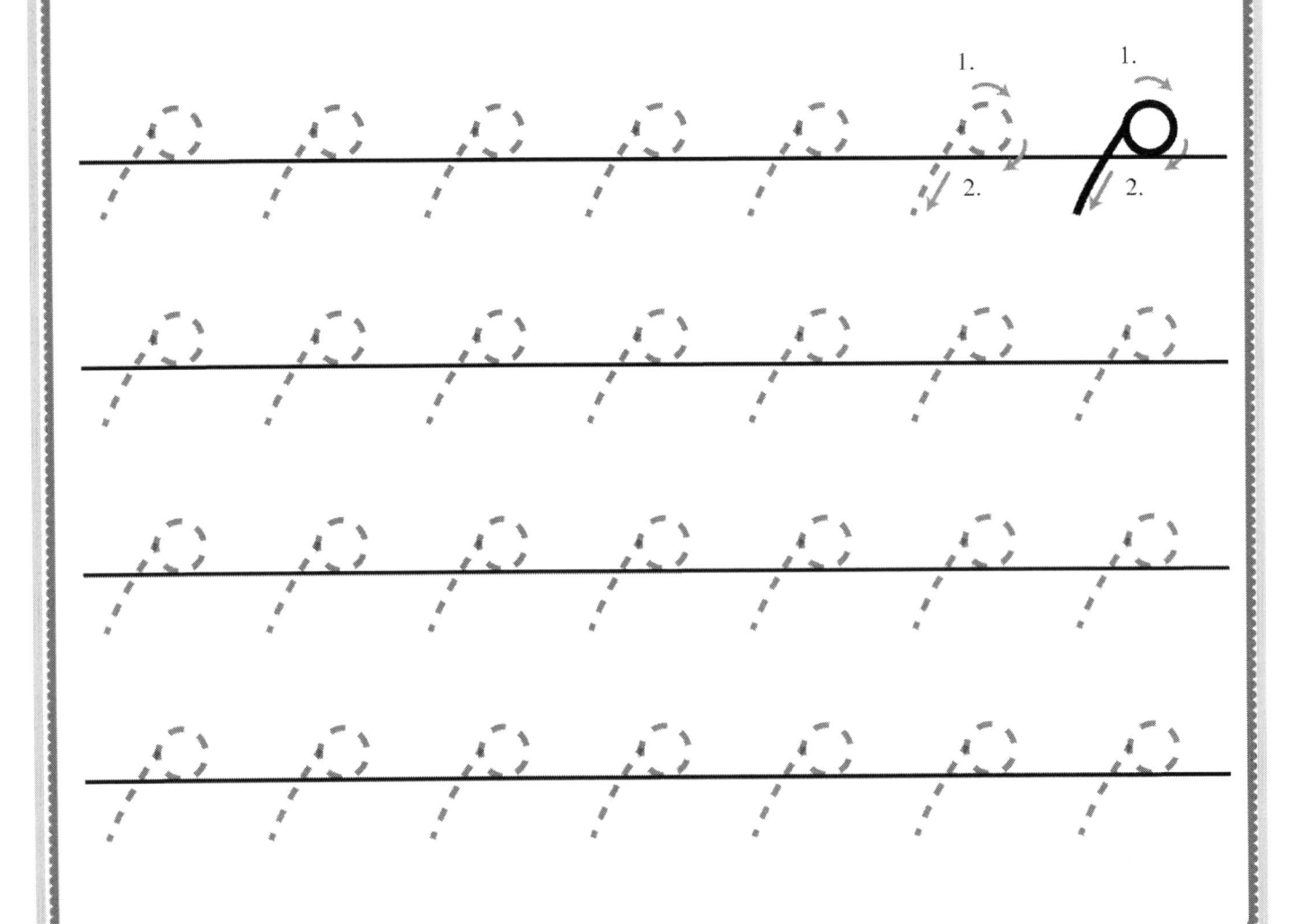

Meem (m)

Guided Practice

Guided Practice

Guided Practice

Guided Practice

Lesson: 25

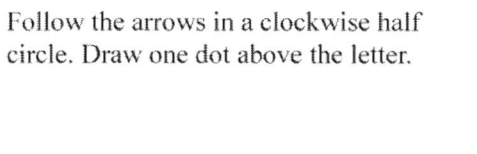

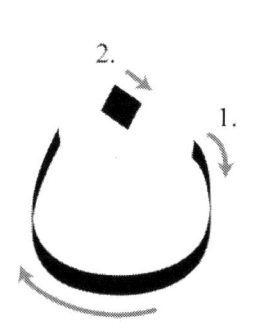

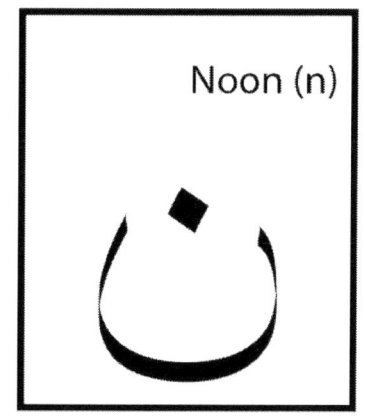

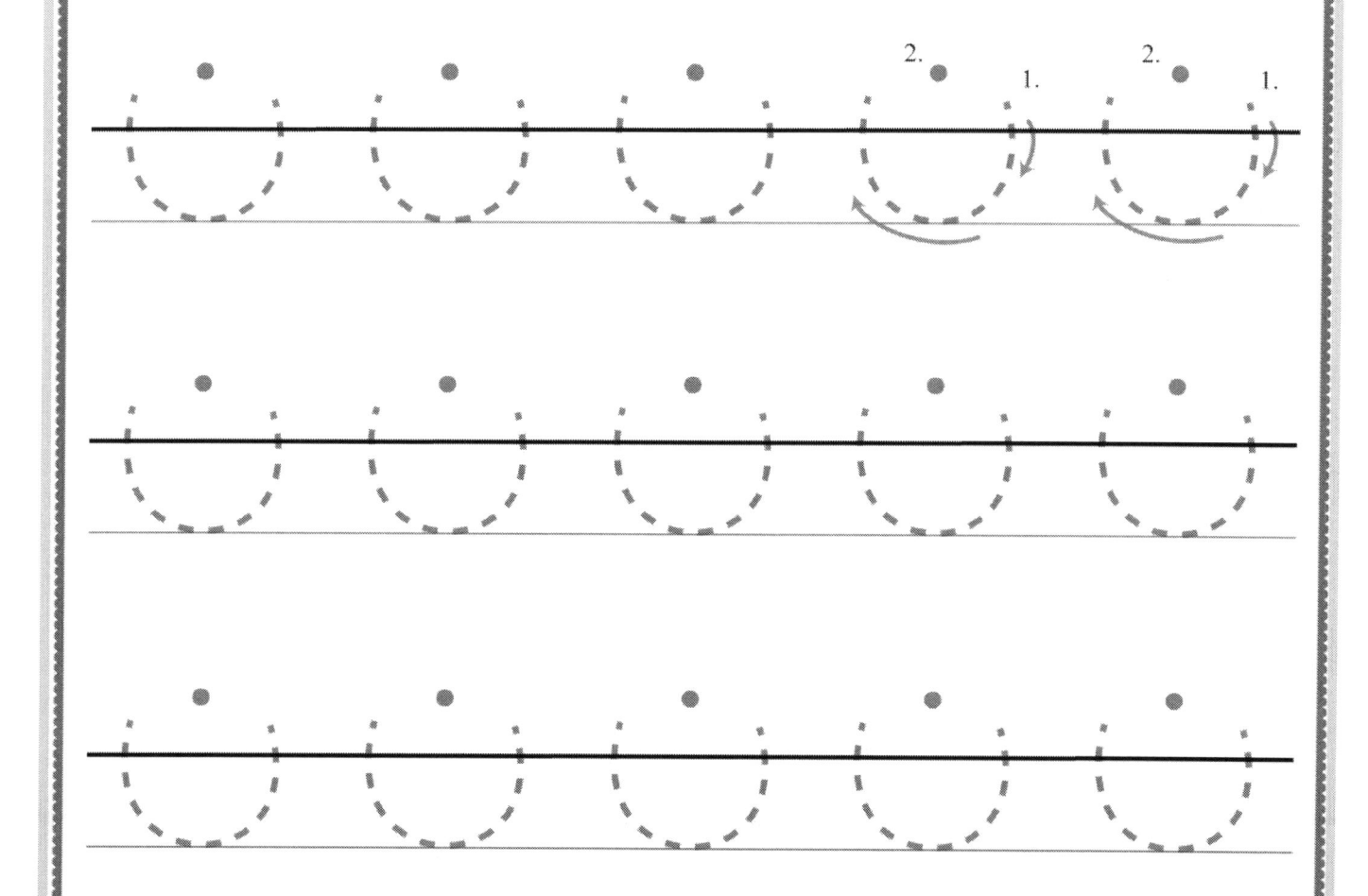

How to write it:
Follow the arrows in a clockwise half circle. Draw one dot above the letter.

Noon (n)

Guided Practice

Guided Practice

Guided Practice

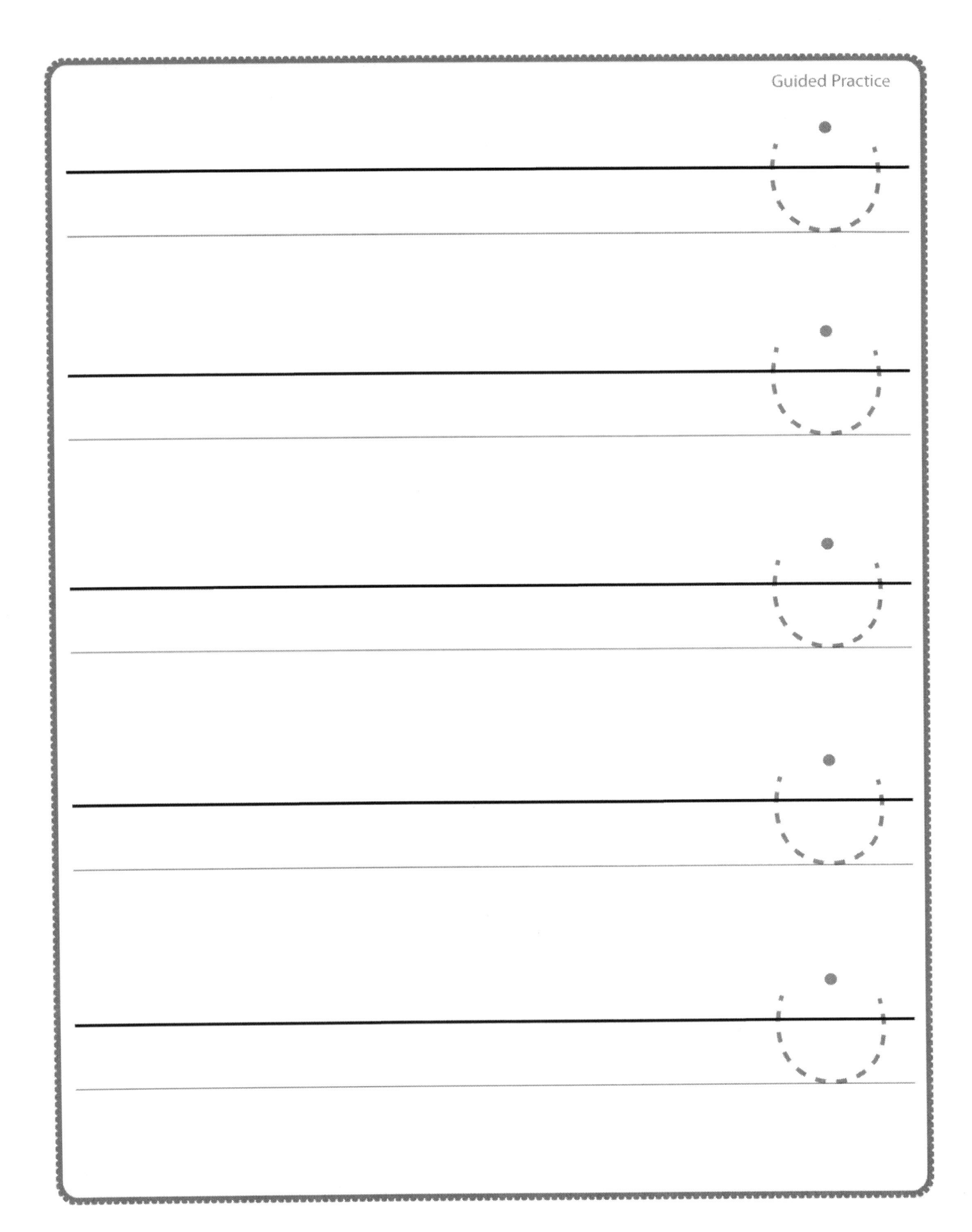

Guided Practice

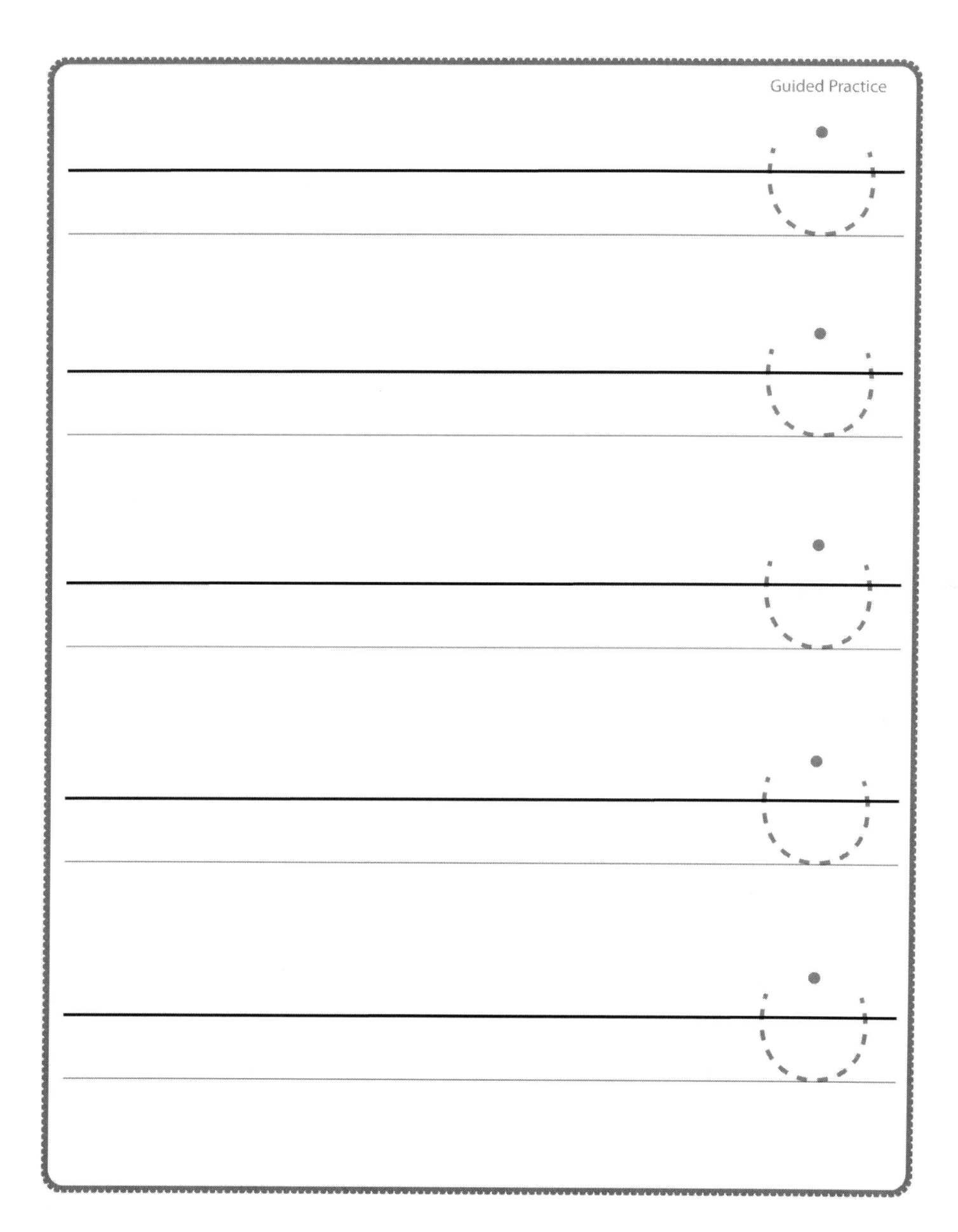

How to write it:
Start at the top of the letter. This letter begins with a swirl and then loops before extending out in a short tail.

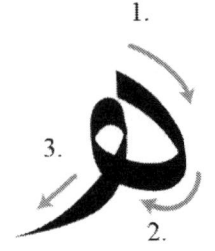

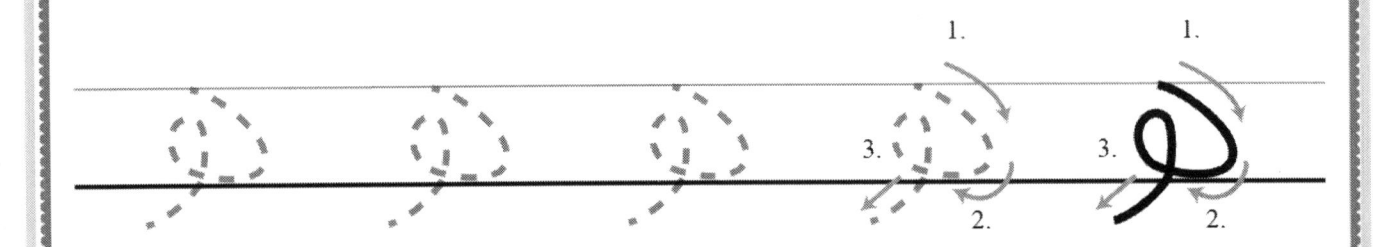

Ha (h)

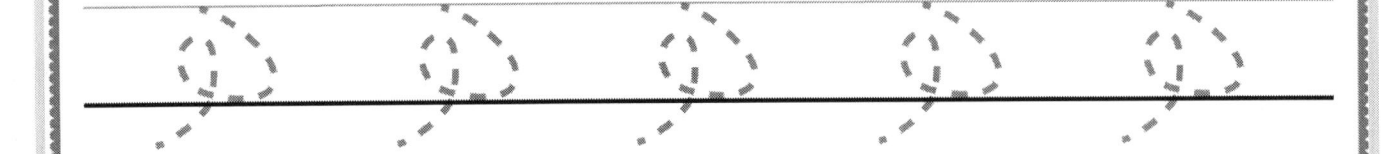

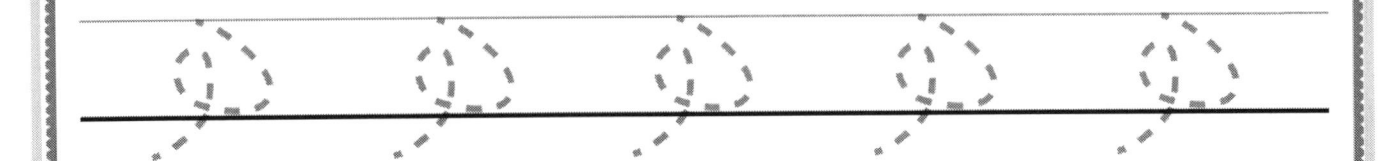

How it's done !

Lesson: 26

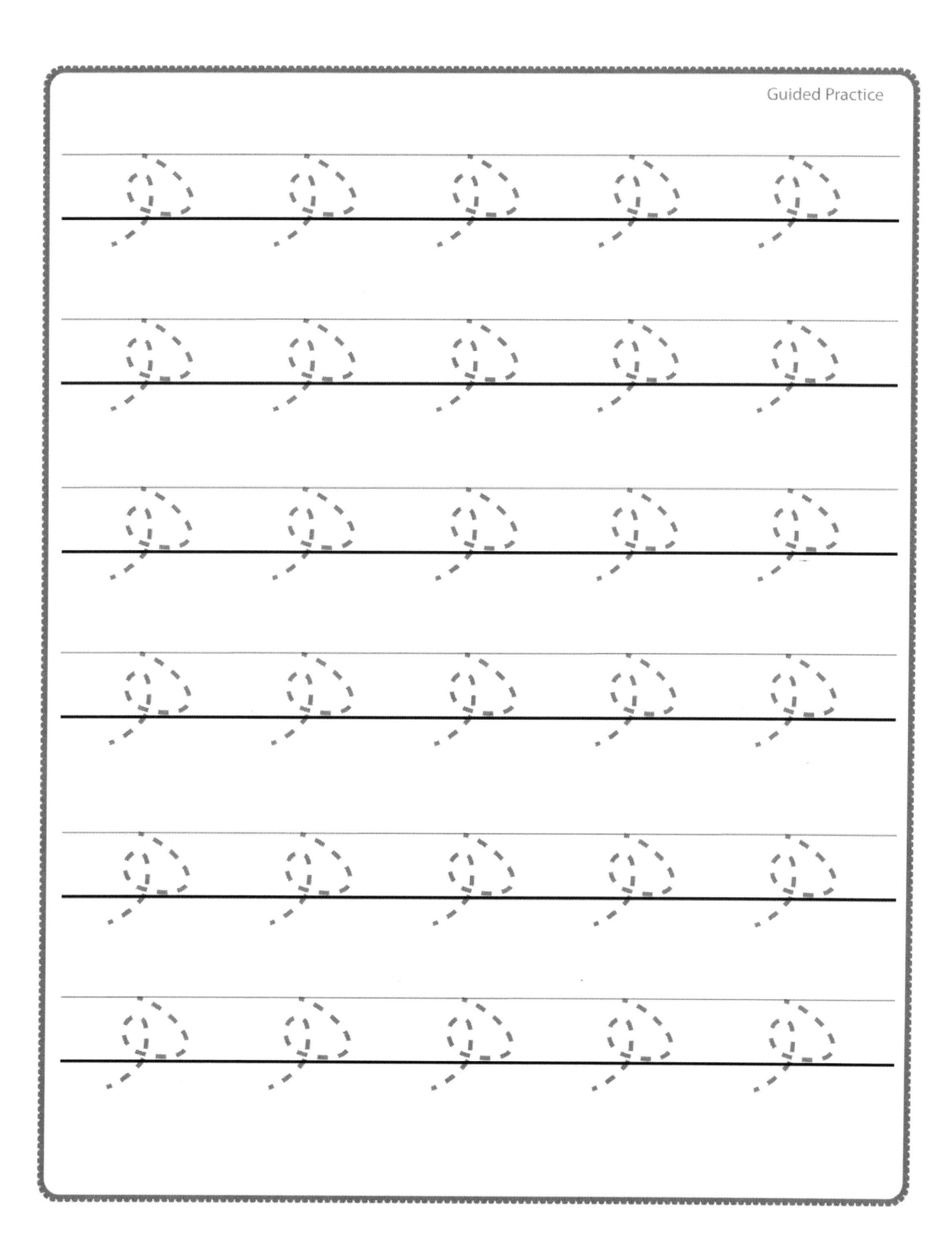

Guided Practice

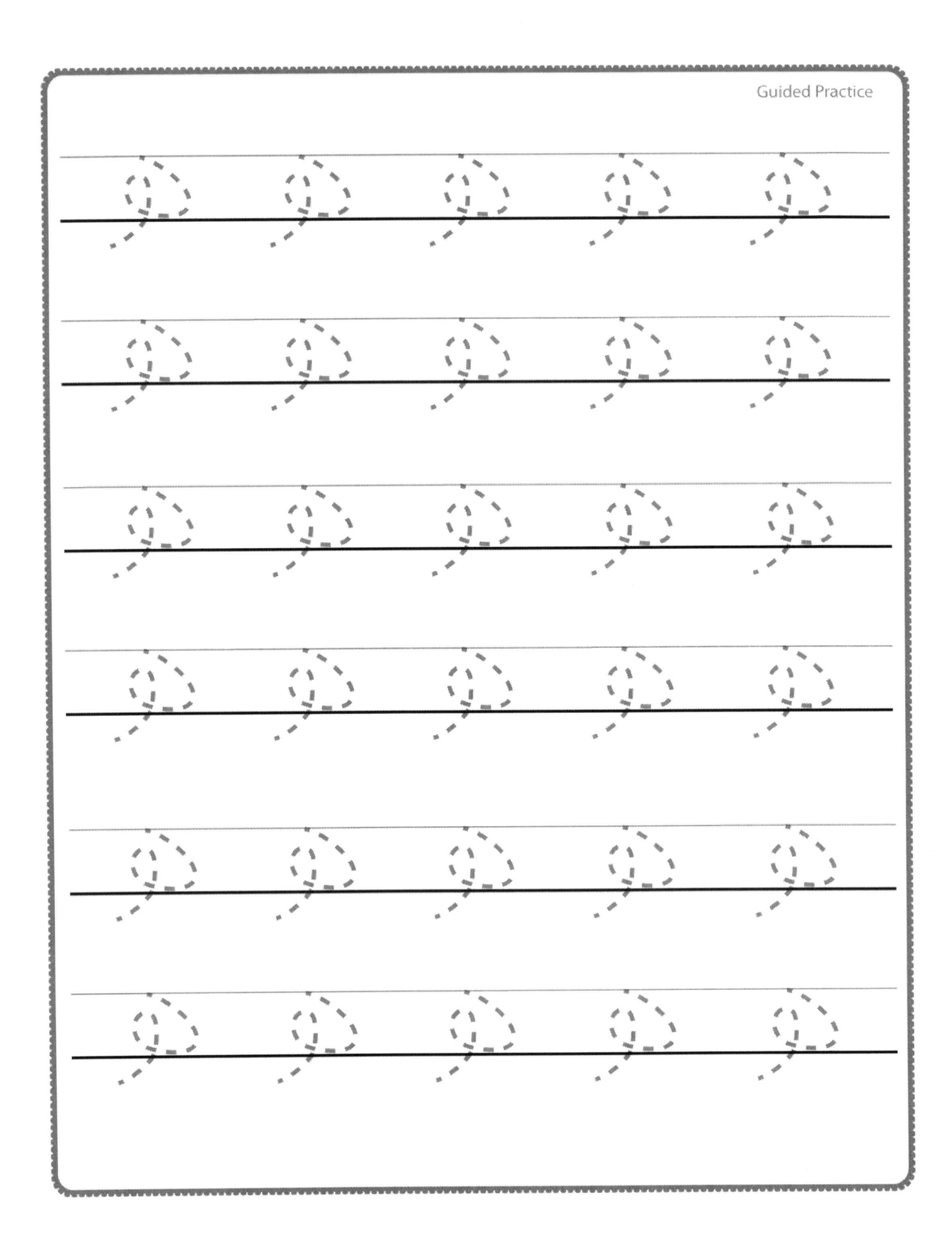

Guided Practice

Guided Practice

Guided Practice

Lesson: 27

How to write it:
Start by drawing a circle. Extend the tail end.

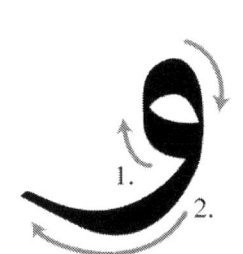

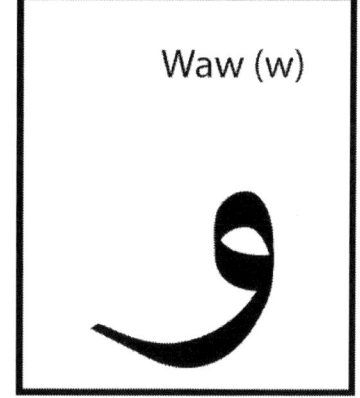

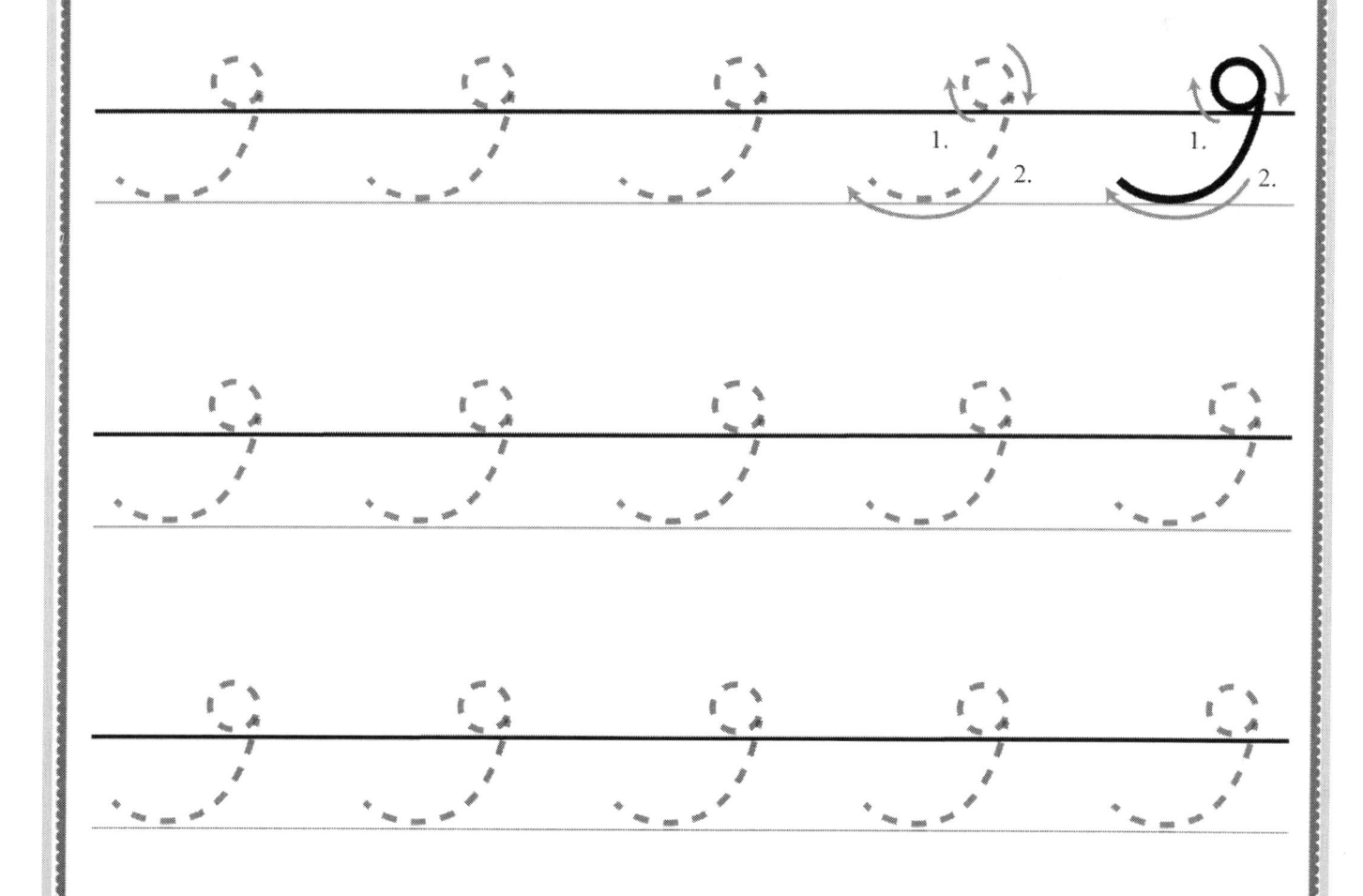

Waw (w)

و

Guided Practice

Guided Practice

Guided Practice

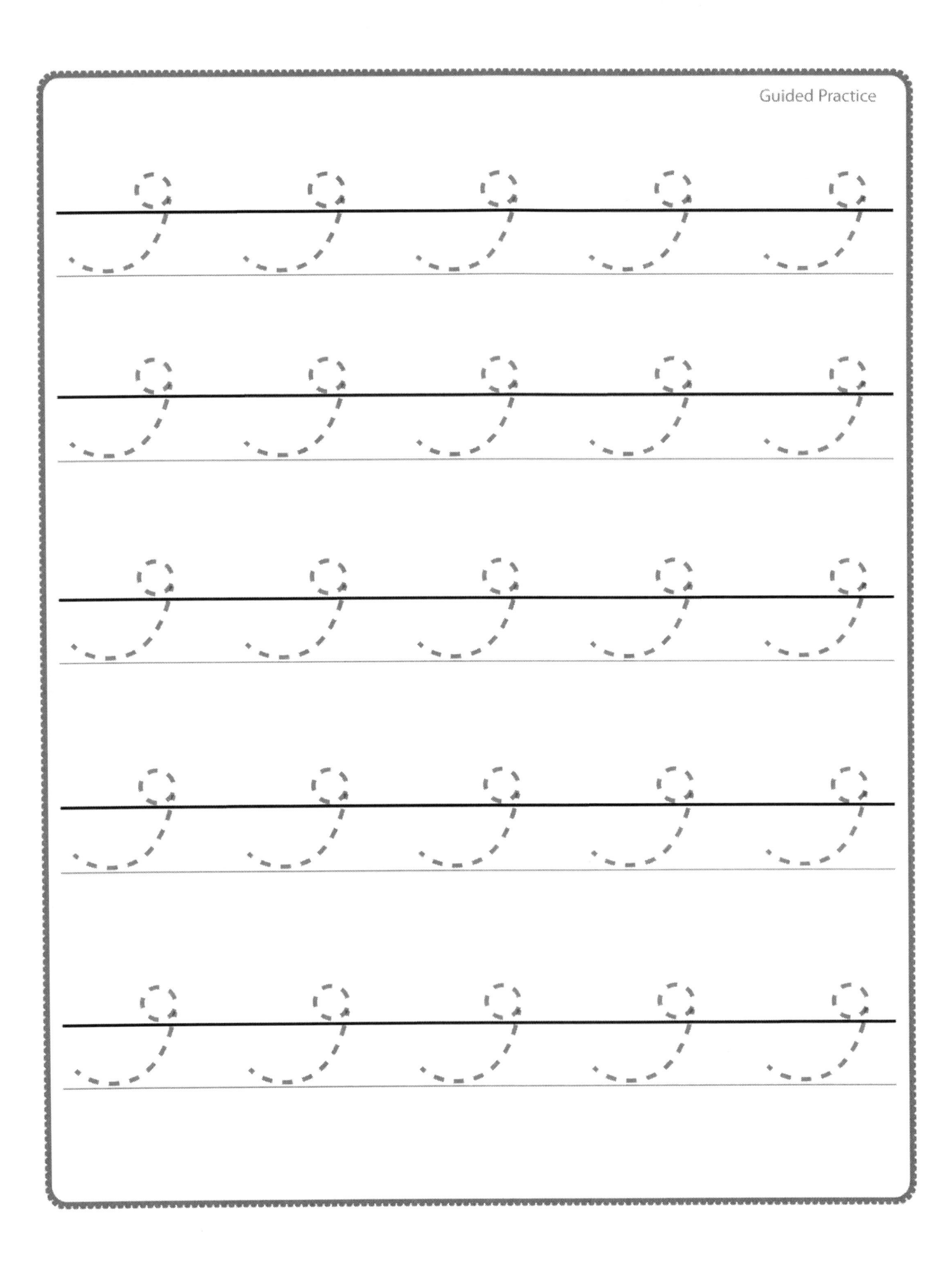

Guided Practice

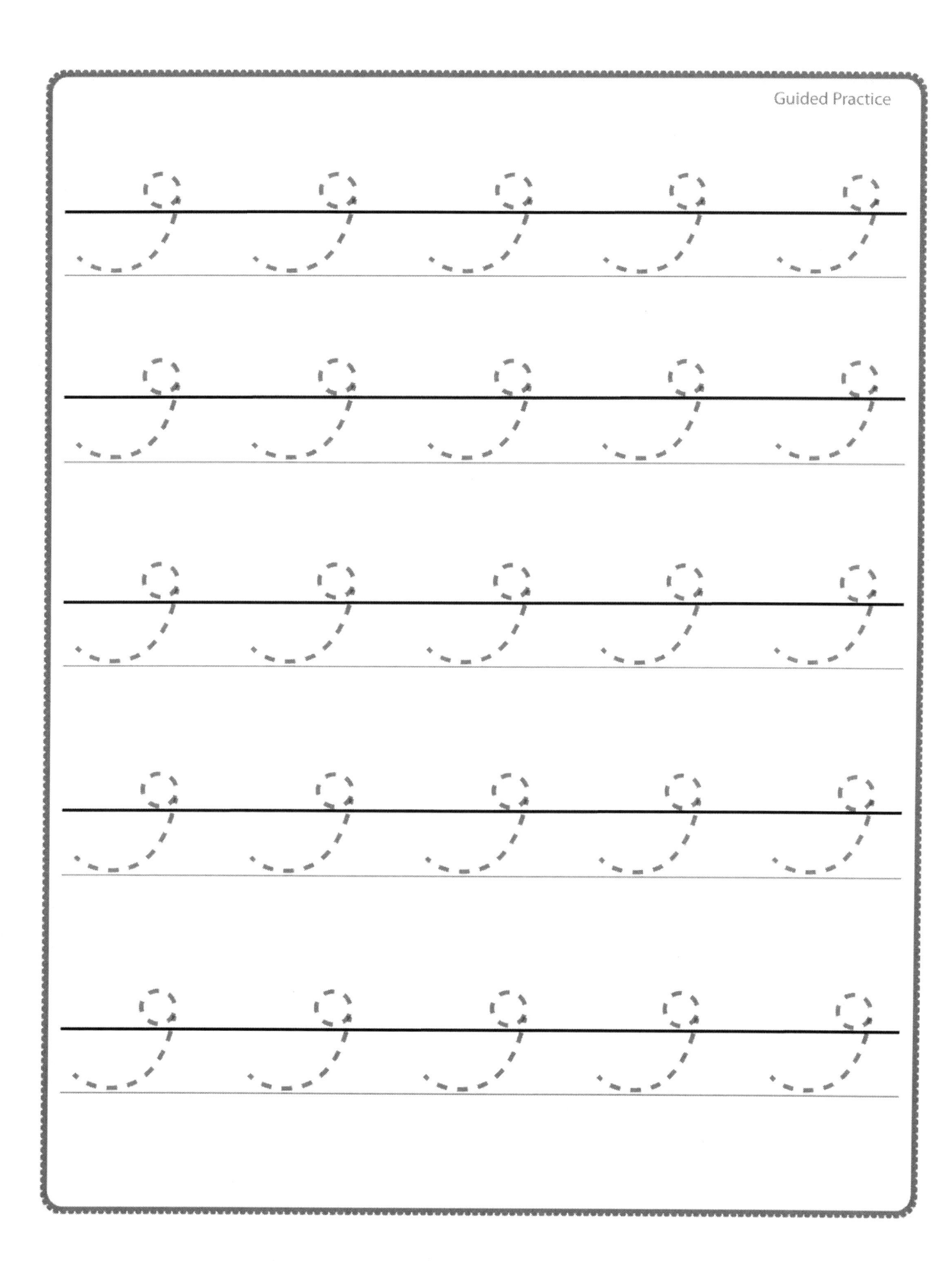

Lesson: 28

How to write it:
The head of this letter rests on the line. Draw the curve of the head and follow the arrows as they swirl around in an s-shaped curve before coming back up.

Yaa (y)

ي

Guided Practice

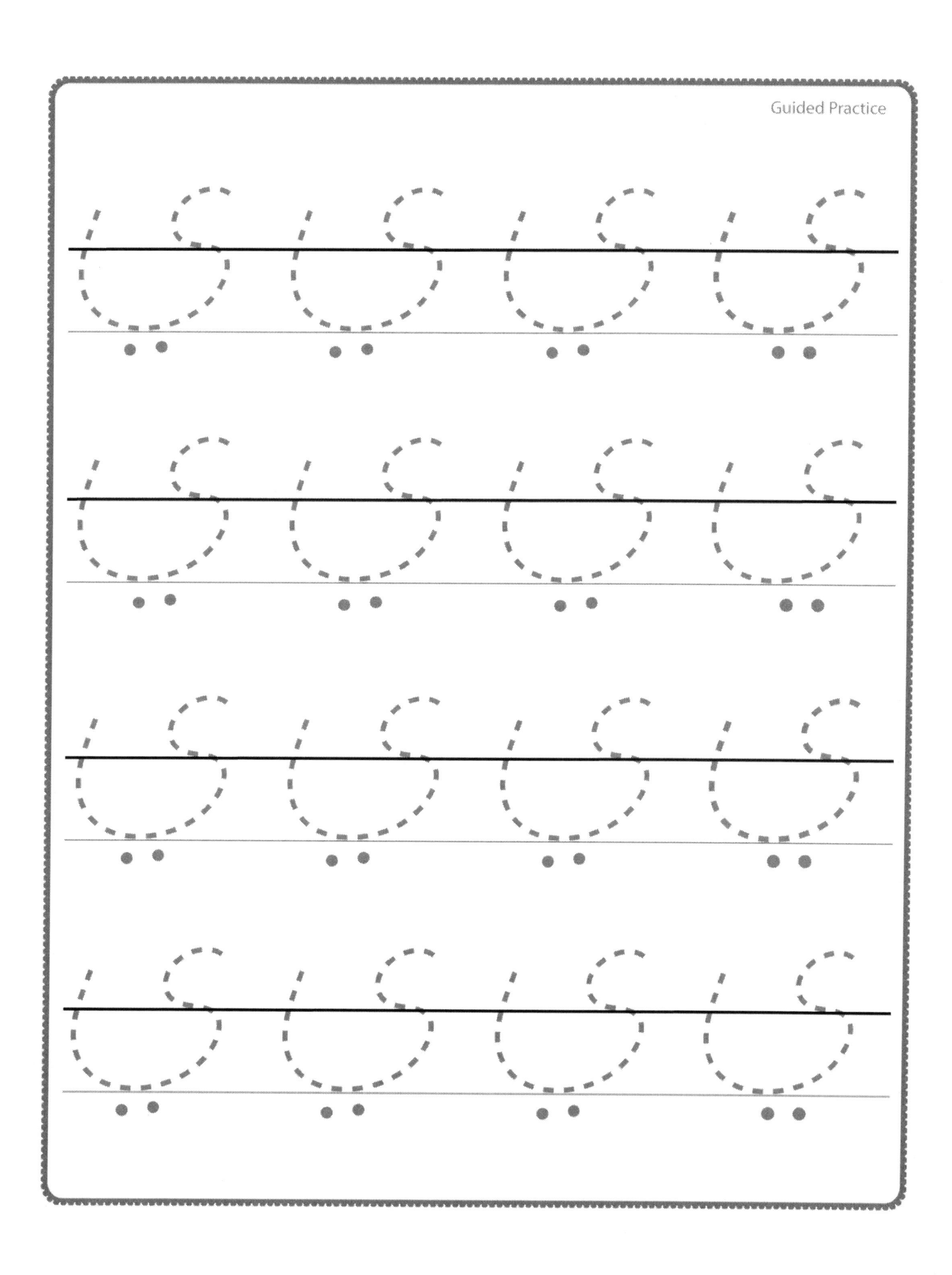

Guided Practice

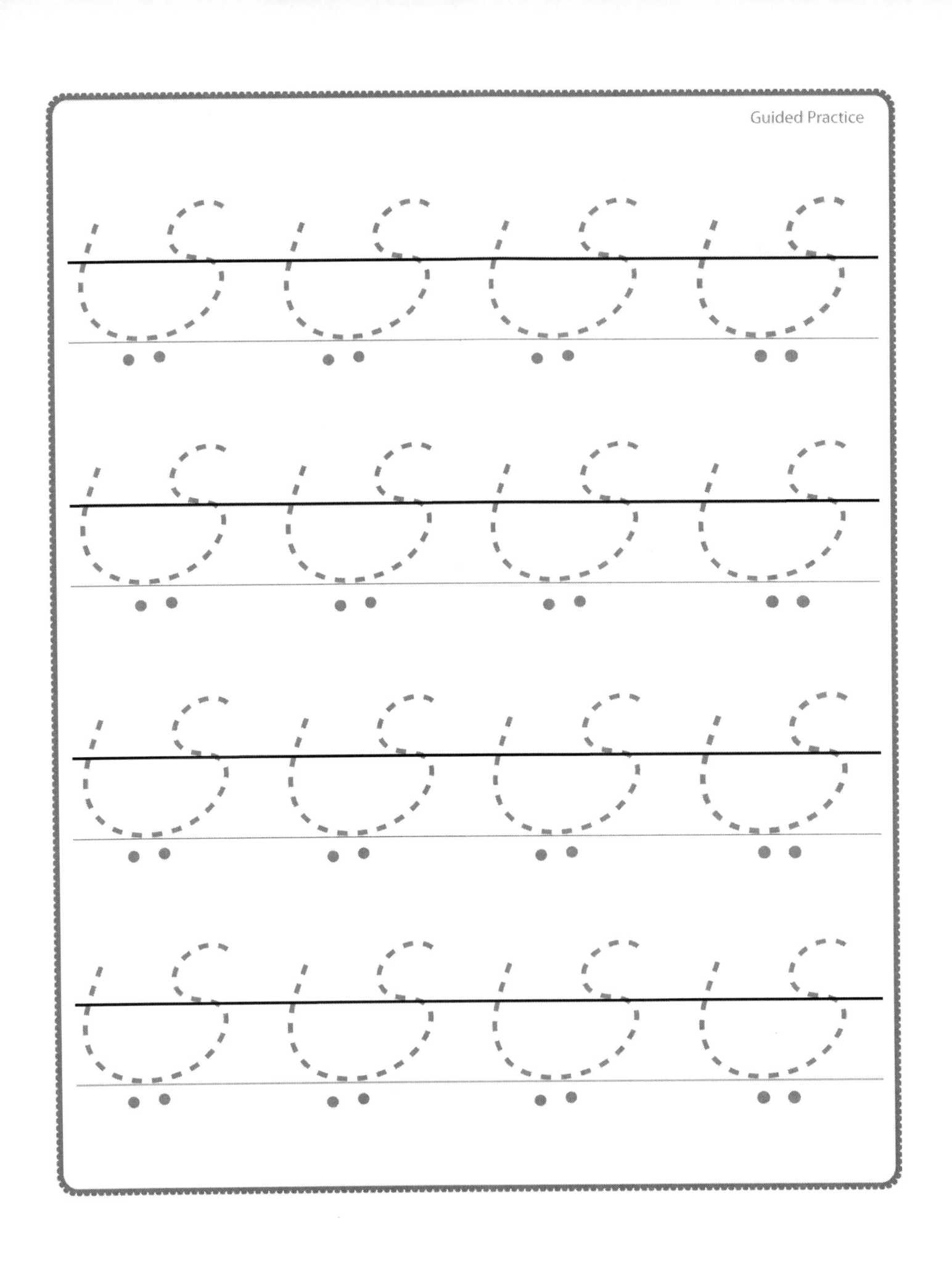

Guided Practice

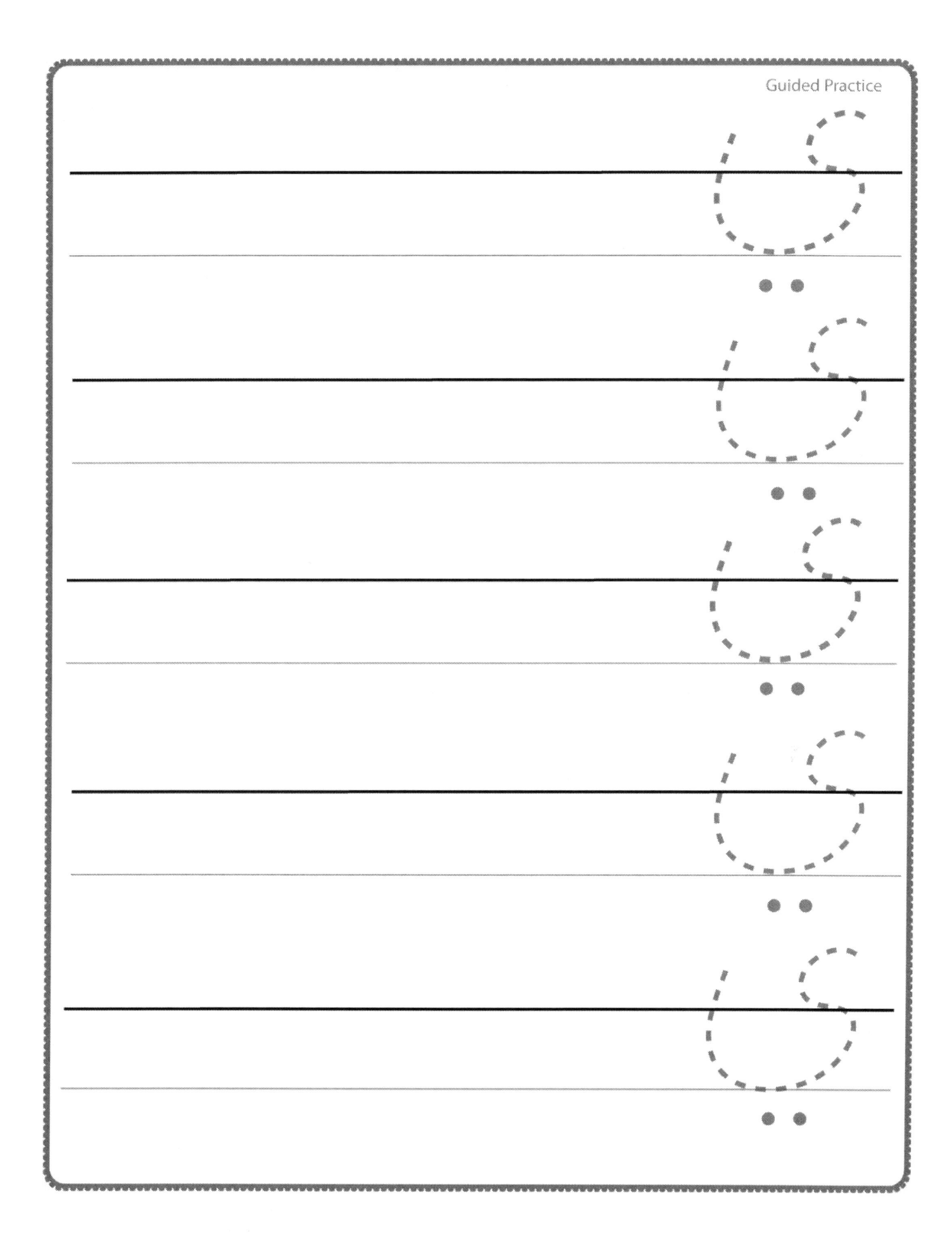

Guided Practice

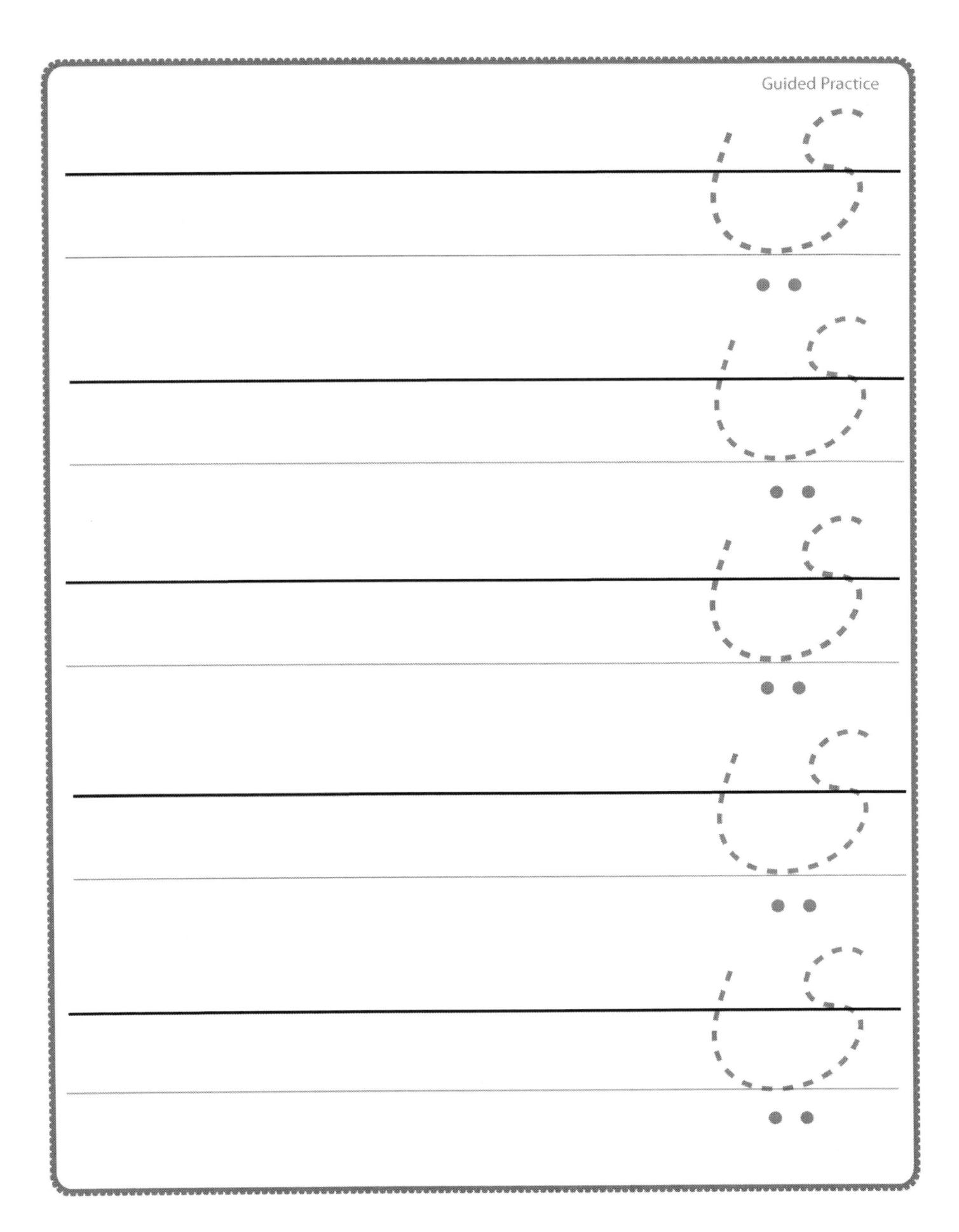

Printed in Great Britain
by Amazon